A SOURCE BOOK OF SHIPS

The great Tea Race of 1866. The Taeping is just ahead of the Ariel as they sail up the English Channel

A SOURCE BOOK OF

SHIPS

Compiled by Laurence Dunn

WARD LOCK LIMITED
LONDON

Text © Ward Lock Limited 1970

First published 1970
Reprinted 1973
Revised and Reprinted 1976

ISBN O 7063 1215 5
WARD LOCK LIMITED, 116 Baker Street, London W1M 2BB

Typeset and originated by Print Origination, Liverpool
PRINTED IN GREAT BRITAIN by Butler & Tanner Ltd., Frome, Somerset

INTRODUCTION

Whereas other forms of transport are comparatively recent in history, ships can almost be said to be as old as history itself, for in essence the first ship was born when prehistoric man, in a moment of daring, sat astride a floating log.

Among the intriguing aspects which come to light during historical research are the surprisingly frequent examples of a parallel of thought, even in widely separated areas. In any description of early ships and types there is the difficulty of terms and their usage which have since become quite outmoded. For example, the use of "burden" (or burthen), let alone its relationship with "tons and tonnage", is of little significance today. Instead, most persons, I hope, have acquired the faculty of using gross tonnage, displacement or deadweight as a means of roughly assessing size in terms of actual dimensions. Even so, gross tonnage differs according to whether it be calculated by British, American, Suez Canal, Panama Canal or other standards. The famous liner UNITED STATES has never been materially altered, yet her gross tonnage, over a relatively short span of time, has varied between 53,329 and 38,216.

The current official use of overall length is logical enough and for most far preferable to that of length between perpendiculars, but centuries back it was length of keel which was so often given. As a result, the size for instance of that first Cunarder, the BRITANNIA, has often been minimised, by the acceptance that the length given conformed to current standards of measurement.

In this book I have aimed at avoiding such misleading over-simplification. Even so there is the occasional unsolved riddle resulting from past ambiguities. In general, over the centuries of sail, details of only the larger or more important ships have survived. Fairly good coverage of Naval vessels has been offset by a virtual void of precise information concerning the humble, average-sized merchant ships. Even so, it is very apparent that, in terms of design, contemporaries of these two categories could be a century apart. This is not really surprising, for today one can, if one seeks them out, travel by paddle steamers whose form of propulsion is not so far removed from that of the COMET, or alternatively, skim the surface by Hovercraft.

Laurence Dunn

CALENDAR OF EVENTS

A.D.527	Bas-relief provides pictorial evidence of Roman warship with ox-driven paddle wheels
1325	Seal of Poole gives first definite indication of a stern rudder
1461	Cannon first recorded on an English ship
1488	Naval vessel REGENT is the first English one to have four masts
1492	Christopher Colombus sails from Spain and discovers the New World
1501	Ports first cut in the actual ship side, so permitting the use of cannon on the lower deck
1566	Opening of Britain's oldest existing artificial waterway, the Exeter Canal
c. 1600	Introduction in English ships of top-masts which can be lowered in bad weather
1600s	Jibs—or equivalent triangular sails—first appear in small craft
1783	The Marquis de Jouffroy d'Abbans' steamboat PYROSCAPHE runs for 15 minutes on the River Saone
1788	John Fitch's paddle steamboat makes 20-mile trip between Philadelphia and Burlington
	Patrick Miller's twin-hulled paddle steamboat runs successful trials
1802	CHARLOTTE DUNDAS tows two 70-ton barges for 19½ miles on the Forth and Clyde Canal
1805	Battle of Trafalgar gives Royal Navy sea supremacy
1807	In America Robert Fulton achieves commercial success with his steamboat NORTH RIVER
1812	COMET opens the first commercial steamboat passenger service in Europe
1819	The SAVANNAH becomes the first steamship to cross the Atlantic, but does so mainly by sail
1822	The AARONMANBY built—the first iron ship to go to sea
1838	SIRIUS becomes the first ship to cross the Atlantic under steam alone, closely followed by the GREAT WESTERN, the first steamship to be expressly built for trans-Atlantic service
1839	Robert Napier introduces an improved form of steeple engine
1840	Early screw ship ARCHIMEDES circumnavigates the British Isles
	BRITANNIA leaves Liverpool for Halifax and Boston, so opening the Cunard trans-Atlantic mail service
1842	The British Navy buys its first screw ship, the 164-ton MERMAID, which it renames DWARF
1845	The GREAT BRITAIN makes her first voyage from Liverpool to New York, becoming both the first screw ship and the first iron one to cross the Atlantic
c. 1850	Introduction of the first water-tube boiler—the Belleville, which in its later modified form was widely used
1852	Introduction of the screw collier
	Cunard buys the BRITISH QUEEN (built 1849)—their first iron and screw ship

1854	The first compound-expansion engine to be fitted in a sea-going ship—the BRANDON
1859	Completion of the GREAT EASTERN, a giant before her time
1860	Launch of H.M.S. WARRIOR, Britain's first iron-built, armoured warship
1861	The brig ELIZABETH WATTS carries the first full cargo of oil (in barrels) from the U.S.A. to Britain
1863	Experimental screw steamer CONNECTOR built, her hull made up of five hinged and detachable sections. A failure, but the concept—of detachable floating cargo-carrying units—is perfected in the 1969 LASH ship
1864	H.M.S. ROYAL SOVEREIGN (launched 1857) converted into Britain's first turret warship
1869	Opening of the Suez Canal—a death blow to sailing ships
1871	The White Star Line, in its first ship, OCEANIC, breaks with tradition by placing the first class accommodation amidships
1872	Gas lighting first introduced, on the White Star ADRIATIC
1873	Screw steamer PROPONTIS, re-engined becomes the first seagoing ship with triple-expansion engines
1878	The ZOROASTER built, the first tanker to be used as such, also notable as being fitted to burn oil fuel
1879	Completion of the CITY OF BERLIN, the first trans-Atlantic ship to have internal electric lighting
1884	The MARTELLO is the first steamer built for the North Atlantic trade to have triple-expansion machinery
1884-5	The UMBRIA and ETRURIA built, the last single-screw express liners for North Atlantic service
1886	Tanker GLUCKAUF launched on the Tyne. Because of her internal design she has become accepted as the prototype of the present-day oil tanker
1888	Re-engined, the PHOENICIAN became the first Atlantic trader to have quadruple-expansion engines
1888	GREAT EASTERN sold for scrap and the new CITY OF NEW YORK, of 10,500 tons gross, becomes the world's largest ship. She is also the first express liner to have twin screws
1889	Her sister CITY OF PARIS becomes the first to average over 20 knots across the Atlantic
1891	The SEINE is one of the very earliest merchant ships to have a cruiser stern
1892	The term "turret ship" is now applied to cargo vessels; Doxfords, of Sunderland launch the TURRET, the first of a new type, of which over 100 were built
1897	The TURBINIA outpaces all at Spithead as she demonstrates the capabilities of turbine propulsion
	With the KAISER WILHELM DER GROSSE Germany regains the Blue Riband after an interval of 20 years
1899	H.M.S. VIPER launched. A destroyer of 31 knots she is the first ship in the Royal Navy to be turbine-driven
1902	The Royal Navy receives its first submarines
1903	Completion of THE QUEEN, the world's first turbine cross-channel ship
	With a deadweight of 12,500 tons the new NARRAGANSET becomes the world's largest tanker

1904	Launch of the VICTORIAN, the first trans-Atlantic turbine liner
	The first motor-tanker, of about 800 tons d.w., is built on the Volga for canal-river use
1906	H.M.S. DREADNOUGHT launched, a turbine driven, all-big-gun battleship which outclasses all others
1907	The Cunard LUSITANIA is completed. The first to exceed 30,000 tons, she is both the world's largest and fastest, also the first quadruple screw liner
1908	LUSITANIA becomes the first to average more than 25 knots across the Atlantic
	The introduction of longitudinal framing—in the PAUL PAIX—brings greater structural strength and makes possible the construction of larger tankers
1909	The White Star LAURENTIC is the first ship to combine reciprocating and turbine machinery
	VESPASIAN (built 1887) is re-engined, becoming the first sea-going ship to have geared turbines
1910	Launch of the VULCANUS, the first sea-going motor tanker. Designed for local service out East
1911	Motor cargo ship TOILER built for service in Canada. The first diesel-propelled ship to cross the Atlantic
1912	A Short biplane flies off the fore-deck of H.M.S. AFRICA, then moored in Sheerness Harbour
	The TITANIC, the world's largest ship, is lost on her maiden voyage
	Danish SELANDIA, 4,963 tons gross, first ocean-going diesel-driven cargo liner, starts her maiden voyage
	The EAVESTONE (1,781 tons gross) launched in May, is Britain's first motor cargo ship
1913	The IMPERATOR (later BERENGARIA) is the first ship to exceed 50,000 tons
	The birth of the super-tanker: SAN FRATERNO, 15,700 tons d.w., is the world's largest
1914	Completion of the AQUITANIA, the last four funnelled liner to be built
	Liner TRANSYLVANIA built—with geared turbines
	The start of World War 1 is soon followed by the introduction of the first aircraft carriers—all conversions.
	Completion of the Panama Canal, although a landslide delays its use until 1915
1917	WAR SHAMROCK, completed at Belfast, is the first British-built standard-type cargo ship
1919	Launch of H.M.S. HERMES, the first British aircraft carrier to be designed as such
1920	The last sailing tanker, the CALCUTTA is withdrawn from trans-Atlantic service
	Completion of the British coaster FULLAGER, the world's first all-welded ship
1921	The first combined oil-ore carrying ship is built in America, the G. HARRISON SMITH, of 14,305 tons gross
1924	The AORANGI enters service—the world's largest motor passenger liner
	The auxiliary schooner BUCKAU is converted in Germany to become the first Rotor ship
1925	The invention of the stern ramp gives great impetus to the use of large whale factory ships
	The Swedish GRIPSHOLM built—the first North Atlantic passenger liner to be diesel-driven

1928	The Maierform hull makes its first appearance, applied to the German trawler WEISSENFELS
1929	ULSTER MONARCH, the world's first cross-channel motorship, enters service
	The North German Lloyd liner BREMEN regains the Blue Riband for Germany after a 23-year interval
	The P & O liner VICEROY OF INDIA is Britain's first large turbo-electric passenger ship
1932	The ISLE OF SARK is the first merchant ship to have activated fin stabilisers (Denny-Brown type)
1935	The Orient Line's ORION introduces a new style profile for passenger ships by having only one mast and a distinctive new livery with corn coloured hull
	The NORMANDIE makes her maiden voyage in May and achieves the first of several record breaking North Atlantic voyages (29.98 knots westwards and 30.31 eastwards)
1936	The QUEEN MARY makes her maiden voyage in May and the QUEEN ELIZABETH is laid down
1938	The Isle of Wight ferry LYMINGTON completed; the first ship with cycloidal (Voith-Schneider) propellers to operate in U.K. waters
	The QUEEN MARY regains the North Atlantic speed record from the NORMANDIE and holds it until 1952
1941	Britain introduces the C.A.M. ship (Catapult Armed Merchant Ship) to help meet the submarine menace
1943	The first M.A.C. ships (Merchant Aircraft Carriers) completed
1945	The present drive-on drive-off ferry concept is initiated by Frank Bustard & Sons' use of L.S.T.s
1946	Britain's final battleship, the VANGUARD, is completed
1949	Withdrawal of the AQUITANIA, the world's last four-funnelled liner
1951	Shell tanker AURIS (built 1948) has one of her two diesels replaced by a gas turbine. Experiments continue for some years before being dropped as not sufficiently encouraging
1952	The liner UNITED STATES wins the Blue Riband and holds it for the rest of her active career
1953	The new TINA ONASSIS, 45,000 tons d.w., gains the tanker size record
	The OLYMPIA becomes the first large trans-Atlantic liner to be built for Greece
1954	The U.S.A. builds the first large ship (of nearly 10,000 tons gross) to carry liquid chemicals
	The first large size (120-ton) Stulcken derrick is fitted in the cargo liner LICHTENFELS
1955	The engines-aft passenger liner SOUTHERN CROSS completed
1956	H.M.S. GIRDLE NESS becomes the world's first guided missiles trials ship
1959	The first tanker to exceed 100,000 tons d.w. is the UNIVERSE APOLLO
1959	SAVANNAH, the world's first nuclear powered merchant ship, is launched
	METHANE PIONEER is converted for the experimental carriage of liquified methane
	The St. Lawrence Seaway is opened

1960	The Grace Line's SANTA ELIANA is converted to become the first American all-container ship designed for non-domestic routes
1960-1	The ORIANA and CANBERRA introduce new standards as regards size and speed to the Australian trade
1961	Twin funnels first appear on tankers, notably those owned by Shell
1962	The FRANCE, the world's longest (and now largest) liner enters service
1965	The keel laying of the QUEEN ELIZABETH 2 takes place in July
1966	The IDEMITSU MARU of 206,000 tons d.w. becomes the world's largest tanker
	The first international hovercraft service (Ramsgate-Calais) is opened by Hoverlloyd
1967	A.C.L., an international consortium, start a new trans-Atlantic container service
	The world's last three funnelled liner, the QUEEN MARY, makes her last voyage
1968	The UNIVERSE IRELAND enters service; first of six tankers, each of over 312,000 tons d.w.
1969	The QUEEN ELIZABETH 2 enters service. The first LASH ship, the ACADIA FOREST, is completed
1969	The UNITED STATES, the world's fastest liner, laid up
1970	Introduction of container ships continues apace
1971	Mercantile application of gas turbines reaches new peak, in four large 26-knot container ships
	With P & O re-grouping the British India, Federal, Hain-Nourse, New Zealand and Strick Lines lose their identity
1972	The SEAWISE UNIVERSITY (ex QUEEN ELIZABETH) destroyed by arson at Hong Kong
1973	Fuel crisis hits all shipping and hastens end of old uneconomic cruise ships
	The GLOBTIK LONDON, 483,939 tons d.w., becomes the world's largest tanker
1974	The FRANCE withdrawn, but build-up of new P & O purpose-built cruise fleet continues
1975	Suez Canal re-opens after eight-year closure
	Japanese nuclear ship MUTSU adrift after accident

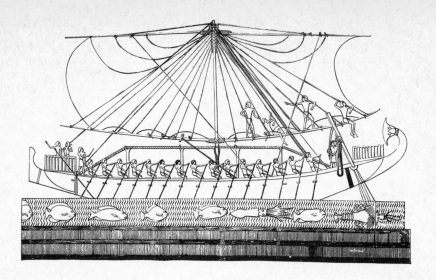

EGYPTIAN SHIP (circa 1600 B.C.): Marshland then being widespread, the very earliest Egyptian boats were made of bundles of papyrus reeds which grew there in profusion. Wood was always scarce, apart from acacia, which could only be used in very short lengths. The wooden boats which followed conformed to the same general shape, and, elegant though they looked in profile, were very shallow and beamy—having a length/beam ratio of about four to one. That shown, one of the much larger sea-going type as used for the trading expedition to Punt, had a length of about 70 ft., its breadth being about 17 ft. and depth 4 or 5 ft. The long steering oar, mounted at the side on a tall post, had a vertical tiller. Structural hull weakness was offset by a hogging truss which was held overhead by vertical struts and attached to both bow and stern. Centuries later a steel equivalent featured on many light draught American steamers

11

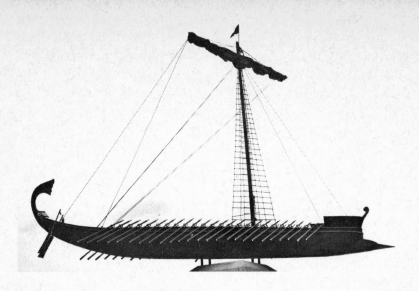

GREEK GALLEY (circa 500 B.C.): In the Mediterranean the galley co-existed with other types for 2,000 years or so. It was essentially oar-propelled, the use of sail being quite secondary. It was doubtless because of this and its lack of cargo space that the galley as a type had so little effect on subsequent designs. Precise details are virtually non-existent and surviving representations are generally too stylised to be really helpful. That illustrated tops a monument in the Greek city of Thessaloniki. Although much simplified, it shows the basic characteristics of the galley, be she large or small. With 25 oars aside in a single bank, this one was probably about 120 ft. long. The very heavy keel was extended forward to form the ram. Otherwise the hull above, long, slim and of no great depth, was of relatively light construction. Larger vessels had several tiers or banks of oars, extra deck width being achieved by the fitting of *parados* or outriggers

ROMAN TRADING SHIP (A.D. 200): In contrast to the galley, this vessel was designed for the carriage of bulk cargoes, typically grain from Egypt. Although many vessels were larger, those intended to navigate the River Tiber were limited to about 75 tons cargo capacity or 80 ft. in length. The hull, deep and beamy, had a length/breadth ratio of around 3 to 1. To ensure ample longitudinal strength it had two or more wales (heavy external timbers) which extended from stem to stern. The hull was virtually double ended and both stem and stern were raked. Over the latter was the swan carving, this customary for merchantmen; just forward of it was a sizeable cabin, while either side of this were projecting galleries which supported twin steering rudders. The rigging of both masts was very efficient. The provision of a secondary mast forward was a notable development, since although the sail it carried was small, it contributed very greatly to the ship's sailing abilities

13

VIKING SHIP (A.D. 900): Viking ships varied in size from small ones intended for local use to large fighting and sea-going units. Others of medium size were built to carry merchandise or livestock. Always they were undecked, built of oak and had clinker (i.e. overlapping) planking. Steering was by means of a single oar placed on the right-hand side of the hull, which in time became known as the steerboard, later starboard, side. Despite their single mast and sail, these ships could sail surprisingly well. When under oar power the mast was lowered, the oars being worked through circular ports cut in the gunwales, openings which were otherwise kept closed. Typical of the medium size type is the Norwegian Gokstad ship which was found in a burial mound near Sandefjord, and is now in an Oslo museum. Estimated as being of 22 tons displacement and having a sail area of 750 sq. ft., it is 77 ft. long, 17 ft. broad and nearly 6 ft. deep

CINQUE PORTS SHIP (A.D. 1300): There is a long and remarkable gap in our knowledge of ships between the 9th century and the early 15th century. Illustrations are largely confined to contemporary seals, but in these, crudity of execution is coupled with grotesqueness of proportion—the artist's obvious aim having been to fill the space available. Again, these seals show only the King's warships or major vessels, not the average traders. Models covering this period are therefore largely based on supposition. That shown is of a type which in a somewhat less elaborately fitted form was long favoured by Western Europe—for only the larger Northern vessels had a forward (fighting) castle. The after castle evolved into an enclosed structure containing accommodation for persons of importance.

In essence, the hull was a deeper, fuller version of the Viking one, its length/breadth ratio being about 3:1. The quarter rudder was a dying feature, giving way to a rudder slung on the stern post

SANTA MARIA (1491). This was the flagship of Christopher Columbus during his famous voyage which led to the discovery of America. She was a nao and in company with the smaller PINTA and NINA—both caravels—she left Spain in August 1492. After exploration in the Bahamas area she grounded—on Christmas day—on a sandbank off Haiti and had to be abandoned. Since she was merely a merchant ship requisitioned for the purpose, contemporary information about her is very scanty. Her length from stem to stern post is estimated at between 81 and 86 ft., and her breadth between 24 and 28 ft.

In the model the strengthening wales (shown varnished) are a prominent feature, while the after castle had by then become part of the hull. The bowsprit carried only a squaresail, the ship's sole fore-and-aft sail being a triangular lateen aft. This most useful borrowing had featured in Arab vessels for several centuries

ELIZABETHAN GALLEON (circa 1600): This model is based on a shipwright's draught, the only 16th century one known to exist in Britain. It is particularly interesting in revealing the gay painting and simplicity of moulding which distinguished Elizabethan ships from those of the Stuart period which had elaborate carving and gilding. The vessel shown was of 684 tons burden. Her main dimensions were: length of keel 100 ft., breadth 38 ft., depth of hold 18 ft. Her overhang forward and aft were 36 ft. and 6 ft. respectively. Special hull features were the length of the after castle and the short forward one, the latter being set well back from the stem and long overhanging beak. On her more important masts she carried topgallant sails over the topsails, lateen sails only on the others. Her armament comprised more than 50 bronze guns, their sizes ranging from the equivalent of 32 pdrs to 6 pdrs

SOVEREIGN OF THE SEAS (1637): This famous ship, launched at Woolwich on 13 October 1637, represented a great advance on earlier ones both in design and size. She was the first large British ship for many years not to be given four masts and the fitting of that number soon ceased. Her sail plan was exceptionally lofty (small royals were set over the topgallant sails on both the foremast and mainmast) and remained unequalled for many years. As built she exceeded her designed draught of 19.5 ft. by 2.7 ft., and to part-remedy this much of her superstructure was cut away in 1651. Initially she was of 1,141 tons burden, her main dimensions being length of keel 127 ft., length overall 232 ft., breadth 46.5 ft., depth of hold 19.3 ft. She originally carried 102 brass guns, these mounted in three tiers, the largest being four stern chasers each weighing 53 cwt. She was rebuilt in 1659 when her name was changed to ROYAL SOVEREIGN, and again in 1685

18

MARY (1660): Britain's first Royal Yacht was presented to King Charles II by the Burgomaster of Amsterdam at the time of the Restoration in 1660. Years earlier, while at Jersey, the King had learned how to sail and when in Holland his fondness for the sport was duly noted. The MARY was similar to one which just before had carried him on the first part of his journey home from Holland and which he had much admired. A typical Dutch State Yacht, she had been intended for their East India Company. Shallow and beamy, she was of 92 tons burden and measured 50 ft. x 18.5 ft., her draught of only 3 ft. being compensated by lee-boards. She carried 8 small guns and was richly decorated with carving and gilt, especially aft and around the state cabin. For figurehead she had a unicorn, while on the stern she bore the Royal Arms of England. Much used, she was finally wrecked in 1675

H.M.S. VICTORY (1778): This first-rate 100-gun ship, famed as Nelson's flagship at the Battle of Trafalgar in 1805, is now preserved at Portsmouth. As was often the case, construction was very protracted, work on her first starting in 1759. After Trafalgar she was twice flagship in the Baltic and, in between, off Spain. Over the years her appearance was several times altered, notably her stern in 1801, while during her next reconstruction, in 1814-16, her beakhead style bow was replaced by a rounded built-up one. However, following her permanent drydocking in 1922, she has been restored to her Trafalgar appearance.

DATA: *Builders: Chatham Dockyard; Launched: 7 May 1765; First Commissioned: 1778; Tonnage (burthen): 2162; Length on gun (lower) deck: 186 ft; Length of keel: 151 ft; Breadth (extreme): 51 ft. 10 ins; Depth of hold: 21 ft. 6 ins; Crew: about 850; Armament: Lower Deck 30-32 pdrs. Upper deck 30-12 pdrs. Middle deck 28-24 pdrs. Quarter Deck 12-12 pdrs. Forecastle 2-12 pdrs and 2-68 pdrs*

28-GUN FRIGATE (circa 1785): Generally the term "frigate" signified a handy vessel capable of sailing fast and mounting anything from 20 to 50 guns. Her niche in the Navy was comparable to that of the pre-1939 cruiser. Over the period 1773-1785 about 30 frigates of the type shown were built for the Navy, and the model most probably represents one of the last of these, H.M.S. ARIEL, which was built at Dover in 1785. The next group of frigates were rather more robust and heavily armed. The ARIEL and her sisters were of approximately 594 tons burden. Their gun deck was 120.5 ft. long, keel 99.5 ft., breadth 33.5 ft. and depth of hold 11 ft. Their complement was about 200. For armament they carried 24-9 pdrs. on the gun deck and four smaller guns on the quarter deck. Special features are the bow shape, lack of build-up aft and the exceptionally long booms aft for the outsize driver

PATRICK MILLER'S EXPERIMENTAL BOAT (1788):
After experiments with manually propelled twin-hulled paddle vessels, an Edinburgh banker named Patrick Miller had the satisfaction of seeing—in 1788—one of his design make the crossing to Sweden. Between its hulls it had five paddle wheels which were worked manually through several capstan and bevel gearings. Its operation proved so exhausting that Miller commissioned William Symington to design a steam engine. This had two vertical cylinders of 4 ins. dia. and

about 18 ins. stroke, and was fitted in one of the twin hulls of a 25 ft. boat, the boiler in the other. Between the hulls were two chain-driven paddles placed in tandem. On 14 October 1787 trials were carried out in Dalwinston Loch, Dumfriesshire, and these fulfilled all expectations, a speed of 5 m.p.h. being attained. After subsequent runs it was decided that further experiments must be more ambitious. The engine was moved to Mr. Miller's house, where it remained until his death in 1815

CHARLOTTE DUNDAS (1802): This, the first really practical steamboat, was built under the direction of a young engineer, William Symington, to test the feasibility of using steam propelled vessels instead of horses to tow barges on the Forth and Clyde canal. Originally it was planned to give her side paddles, but to reduce the risk of wash eroding the canal banks a stern wheel was finally adopted. Boiler and engine were placed abreast each other, the latter (on the port side) driving the wheel by means of a connecting rod and crank, as used in the later engines.

The CHARLOTTE DUNDAS proved able to pull two 70-ton barges a distance of 19½ miles in six hours, but local opposition was such that she had to be laid up—her remains being eventually scrapped in 1861.

DATA: *Builder: A. Hart, Grangemouth; Date: 1802; Owner: Lord Dundas; Length: 56 ft; Breadth: 18 ft; Engine: 10 n.h.p., one horizontal double-acting cylinder, 22 ins. dia., 48 ins. stroke*

COMET (1812): Famed as the first steamboat to operate on a regular passenger service this side of the Atlantic, the COMET was owned by a hotel proprietor at Helensburgh. She first operated between Glasgow and Greenock, making three trips weekly in each direction. This proving unprofitable, she was used for coastal trips and for a while plied on the Firth of Forth. In 1819, after being lengthened and given new engines, she commenced sailing between Glasgow and Fort William. She was on one such voyage on 13 December 1820 when she was wrecked on Craignish Point. The picture shows the replica built for the celebrations 150 years later.

DATA: *Owners: Henry Bell, Helensburgh; Builders: John Wood, Port Glasgow; Launched: 24 July 1812; Completed: 15 August 1812; Tonnage (displacement): 21½ tons; Length overall: 44 ft. 11 ins. (later 65 ft. 6ins.); Breadth: 11 ft. 3 ins; Depth: 6 ft. 4 ins; Draught: 3 ft. 9 ins; Speed: about 6 knots; Engine: Single cylinder, DA, side-lever, jet condensing, cyl. 12½ ins. dia., 16 ins. stroke. About 10 b.h.p. One horizontal boiler, 7 p.s.i. boiler starboard side, engine port side*

SAVANNAH (1818). As the first steam propelled ship to cross the Atlantic, the SAVANNAH achieved lasting fame, but no fortune for her owners. Designed as a sailing ship, she was bought and given auxiliary power while building. She left Savannah in ballast, without passengers, and for sale, on May 24, 1819—bound for Liverpool. She arrived 29 days later, after steaming for less than 90 hours. Finding no buyer there or in the Baltic, she returned to Savannah. Auctioned and stripped of her machinery, she traded coastwise as a sailing ship until wrecked off Long Island in 1821.

DATA: *Owners: Savannah Steam Ship Co; Builders: Fickett & Crockett, East River, New York; Launched: 22 August 1818; Tonnage (burthen): 320; Length between perps: 98.5 ft; Breadth: 25.9 ft; Depth of hold: 14.2 ft. Draught: 13 ft; Speed: 5¼ knots, steam only. (9-10 knots sail only, fresh winds); Passengers: 32 berths; Engines: One single cylinder. 40 $\frac{3}{8}$ in. dia., 60 in. stroke, 90 l.h.p. Boiler pressure from 2 to 5 p.s.i; Fuel: coal or wood*

ENTERPRISE (1825): To India by steam is feasible—such was the intended aim of this small wooden paddler. She was bought, while still building, by a syndicate to compete for a prize offered in India for the first steamer to reach there within a stipulated time. She left Falmouth in August 1825 with 17 passengers, and reached Calcutta 113 days later. Of the period actually spent at sea, she used steam for about two-thirds of the time. Her passage however was far longer than expected. Later owned in turn by the Bengal Government and the East India Company, she proved very useful. For some years she carried the Indian mail to Suez.

DATA: *Owners; Lieut. J.H. Johnston & others; Builders: Gordon & Co., Deptford; Completed: 1825; Tonnage: 470; Length overall: 133 ft; Breadth: 27 ft; Depth: 16.5 ft; Speed: about 7 knots under steam only, Engines: Side-lever type, by Maudslay. 2 cyls., 42 ins. dia., 48 ins. stroke. One copper flue-type boiler. Approx. 3 p.s.i.*

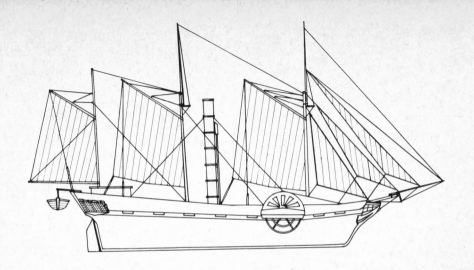

CURACAO (1825): Intended for service between England, North America and the West Indies, this wooden paddle steamer was sold in 1826 and became instead the CURACAO, the first steamship in the Dutch Navy. In April-May 1827 she crossed from Holland to Paramaribo—about 4,000 miles—in 28 days, her machinery being used intermittently. Boiler leaks and broken paddle floats caused difficulty, also inadequate paddle immersion, as freeboard increased with the consumption of fuel. After making two more round Atlantic crossings she had a spell of home service. She returned to the Indies in 1840 and was scrapped ten years later.

DATA: *Previous name: CALPE; Owners: Dutch Navy; Builders: J.H. & J. Duke, Dover; Launched: September 1825; Tonnage (gross): 438; Length between perps: 127.3 ft; Breadth: 26.9 ft; Depth of hold: 16.5 ft; Draught: 13.5 ft; Speed: 8 knots (normal); Crew: 42; Engines: Side-lever type (by Maudslay). 2 cyls. 40 in. dia. 48 in. stroke. Approx. 150 l.h.p. 1 boiler, 3 p.s.i; Armament: 5-36 pdrs., 2-6 pdrs*

SIRIUS (1837): This was the first ship to cross the Atlantic under continuous steam power. Although only designed for short sea routes, she made two round voyages to New York as a substitute for a much delayed new ship. Hitherto salt water for boilers had been the rule, but the SIRIUS was freed from this hazard, fresh water being provided by condensers. With many passengers on board she left Cork on April 4, 1838 and received a tumultuous welcome when she reached New York 18 days 10 hours later, beating the much larger GREAT WESTERN by hours. She was wrecked in 1847 while on a coastal voyage.

DATA: *Owners: St. George Steam Packet Co; Builders: Robert Menzies & Son, Leith; Completed: 1837; Tonnage (gross): 703; Length between perps: 178.4 ft; Breadth: 25.8 ft. (47.3 over paddles); Depth: 18.3 ft; Draught: 15 ft; Speed: 9 knots; Crew: 35; Engines: Side-lever type, 2 cyls. 60 in. dia. 72 ins. stroke. 320 l.h.p. 5 p.s.i.*

GREAT WESTERN (1837): The first ship to be specially designed for regular transatlantic service, the GREAT WESTERN proved outstandingly successful. Built of wood, but immensely strong, she was designed by Mr. I.K. Brunel. Her saloon, 75 ft. long, was the largest and most luxurious yet fitted on any ship.

On her maiden voyage from Bristol she reached New York on 23 April, 1838 (four hours after the SIRIUS) after a passage of 15 days 5 hours. After constant service on this route, she was sold to the Royal Mail S.P. Co., and spent ten years on the W. Indies trade before being scrapped.

DATA: *Owners: Great Western Steam Ship Co; Builders: William Patterson, Bristol; Launched: 19 July 1837; Tonnage (gross): 1320; Length between perps: 212 ft; Breadth: 35.4 ft. (58.3 ft. over paddles); Depth of hold: 23.2 ft; Draught: 16.7 ft; Speed: 8.8 knots (average); Crew: 60; Passengers: 120 first, 20 second; Engines: Side-lever type; 2 cyls. 73.5 in. dia., 84 in. stroke. 750 i.h.p. 4 boilers*

ARCHIMEDES (1838): This was one of the first screw driven ships to be built in Britain. Earlier, F.E. Smith had demonstrated the newly invented propeller with a screw launch—the FRANCES SMITH of 1863—which he tried out on the Paddington canal. He sold his patents to the Ship Propeller Co., who built the much larger ARCHIMEDES as a demonstration vessel. The superiority of the screw was well shown in 1840, when she circumnavigated the British Isles. Her screw was several times modified. It was 7 ft. in diameter and as first fitted was 10 ft. (one complete turn) long. Finally it was two-bladed, with a pitch of 10 ft. Later the ARCHIMEDES had her engines removed and traded as a sailing ship.

DATA: *Owners: The Ship Propeller Company; Launched: November 1838; Tonnage (burthen): 240; Length overall: 125 ft; Length between perps: 107 ft; Breadth: 22.5 ft; Depth: 13 ft; Draught: 10 ft; Speed: 8 knots; Engines: 2 cylinder, 37 in. diameter, 36 in. stroke. 26 r.p.m. 80 n.h.p;*

BRITANNIA (1840): The first of four wooden paddle steamers constructed for Mr. Samuel Cunard's new Liverpool—Halifax and Boston service, her sisters were named ACADIA, CALEDONIA and COLUMBIA. She made her first crossing to Boston in 14 days 8 hours. Her paddles, 28 ft. in diameter, worked at 16 r.p.m. Cargo capacity was 225 tons. For passengers there was a deck saloon aft which had two long fore and aft dining tables; the staterooms and a ladies' cabin being below. Cows were carried for their milk. After making 40 Atlantic crossings, the BRITANNIA was sold to Germany in 1849.

DATA: *Owners: British & North American R.M.S.P. Co; Builders: Robert Duncan & Co., Greenock; Maiden voyage: 4 July 1840; Tonnage (gross): 1156; Length overall: 228 ft; Breadth: 34.3 ft. 56 ft. over paddle boxes; Depth: 24.3 ft; Draught: 16.8 ft; Speed: 10 knots; Crew: 89; Passengers: 115; Engines: Side-lever type, 740 I.h.p; 2 cyls. 72 in. dia., 82 in. stroke. 4 boilers, 9 p.s.i.*

31

GREAT BRITAIN (1843): The GREAT BRITAIN was both the first screw propelled ship to cross the Atlantic, and the first iron hulled one to do so. She left Liverpool on 26 July 1845 for New York, carrying over 600 tons of cargo and some 60 passengers. Her passage took just under 15 days, average speed being 9.3 knots. Iron construction prevented her loss in 1846 when she grounded in Dundrum Bay. Eventually salved, sold and re-engined, she saw long service on the Australian trade. In 1882 she became a sailing ship, her active career ending in 1886 when through stress of weather she sought refuge in the Falkland Islands.

DATA: *Owners: Great Western Steam Ship Co., Bristol; Builders: W. Patterson & Sons, Bristol; Launched: 19 July 1843; Tonnage (gross): 3270; Length overall: 322 ft; Breadth: 50.5 ft; Depth of hold: 32.5 ft; Speed: 11 knots (trials); Passengers: 360; Engines: One, four cylinders, 88 in. dia., 72 in. stroke. 1500 l.h.p. 1 boiler, 15 p.s.i.*

UNITY (1848): This collier brig was typical of the many engaged in that centuries old trade, the carriage of coal to London from North East Coast ports. Like so many of the Geordie brigs she had no figurehead, but the Bentinck Boom was a characteristic fitting. This was a horizontal spar which gave maximum spread to the fore-course—the lowest of the forward square sails. These vessels had large crews and sail expanse, but hull lines were so bluff that few could make the round trip in less than a month. Traffic was such that by the 1840s collier arrivals in the Thames numbered well over 10,000 per year. Bad weather brought many delays, a coal famine being followed by an enormous bunching of colliers which created great congestion in the river.

DATA: *Built: at Whitehaven; Launched: 1848; Gross Tonnage: 190; Length between perps: 91.2 ft; Breadth: 18.5 ft; Depth of hold: 13.9 ft.*

H.M.S. GREENOCK (1849): The largest iron warship of her day, she was provisionally named PEGASUS, but was renamed before launching. She had a telescopic funnel and lifting screw, so that in fair winds she could use sail alone. After having second thoughts about the use of iron warships, the Admiralty sold her in 1852 to the newly formed Australian Royal Mail S.N. Co. Renamed MELBOURNE, she made one round voyage to Australia. Outwards, with 150 passengers, she had many troubles. Homewards, her original and her spare propellers both dropped blades. The fitting—at sea—of a Jury propeller was followed by engine fracture, so she had to sail home. Sold, she did better as a sailing ship.

DATA: *Builders: Scott & Sons, Greenock; Launched: 30 April 1849; Tonnage (burden): 1,413; Length overall: 213 ft; Breadth: 37.3 ft; Depth of hold: 23 ft; Speed: 9.6 knots (trials); Engines: 2-cylinder, with gearing, 719 l.h.p; Armament: 6-8 in., 4-32 pdr. guns*

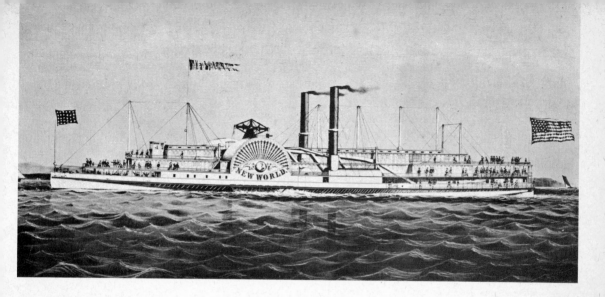

NEW WORLD (1849): This Hudson River steamer, designed for service between New York and Albany, was considerably larger than any hitherto built for inland waterways. She impressed local travellers, not only by her great size, but also by her elaborate fittings. According to one, you could dine on board "as pleasantly as at a Parisian café". After some years on the day service, she was reconstructed for use as a night boat. Besides being widened by 7 ft., she was given two tiers of state rooms above the main deck.

In 1859 she sank after her gallows beam fractured, this forcing the connecting rod through her bottom. Salved and repaired, she was dismantled in 1864.

DATA: *Owners: The People's Line Builders: W.H. Brown, New York; Launched: 1848; Entered Service: June 1849; Tonnage (gross). 1418 (later 1675); Length overall: 371 ft; Breadth: 36 ft; Depth of hold: 10 ft. 6 ins; Speed: Over 18 knots; Engines: Vertical beam type; one cylinder, 76 ins. diameter, 15 ft. stroke*

JOHN BOWES (1852): Famed as the first screw collier, this iron hulled steamer entered service in July 1852. She was designed to speed up and cheapen the transport of coal from the Tyne to London. A success from the first, she could make the round trip in 5 days and carry 650 tons, for which two sailing colliers would have needed a month. She is shown here after her original clipper stem had been altered. Sold in 1898, she was owned first in Norway, then Sweden and Spain. As the VILLA SELGAS and laden with ore, she foundered in a gale in November 1933.

DATA: *Owners: Iron Screw Collier Co; Builders: Paliner Bros. & Co., Jarrow; Launched: 30 June 1852; Tonnage (gross): 437; Length between perps: 150.0 ft; Breadth: 25.7 ft; Depth: 15.6 ft; Speed: 9 knots; Engines: Originally 2-35 h.p. steam engines geared to one shaft. Re-engined 1864 and 1883. Finally compound; Screws: One*

HIMALAYA (1853): The wonder ship of her time, and by far the largest steamer afloat, the HIMALAYA was designed for the London-Alexandria section of the P. & O.'s Eastern mail service. She was converted from paddle to screw propulsion while building, the Admiralty having previously vetoed anything but paddles. She proved exceptionally fast and on occasion, under sail and steam, she logged 16½ knots. With the Crimean War she was first chartered and then bought to become a Naval Transport, and she continued as such until the 'eighties. Thereafter a coal hulk, she was bombed and sunk at Portland in 1940.

DATA: *Owners: P. & O. Steam Navigation Co; Builders: C.J. Mare & Co., Blackwall; Launched: May 1853; Maiden voyage: January 1854; Tonnage (gross): 3,438; (Displacement): 4.690 tons; Length: 340 ft; Breadth: 46.2 ft; Depth of hold: 34.9 ft; Draught: 21.4 ft; Speed: 14 knots; Passengers: 200 saloon; Engines: 1 set, trunk type, 2,050 I.h.p; Screws: One (two bladed)*

37

H.M.S. MARLBOROUGH (1855): The fourth of her name, this wooden first rate line-of-battle ship was laid down in 1850 as a sailing vessel, but while still on the stocks was converted to auxiliary screw propulsion. Her engines were by Maudslay and she had a two-bladed propeller of 19 ft. diameter, which could be lifted when not in use. In 1878 she became a training ship and in 1904 was renamed VERNON II. Sold to breakers in 1924, she was in tow off Brighton when she broke in two and capsized.

DATA: *Builders: Portsmouth Dockyard; Launched: 31 July 1855; Tonnage (displacement): 6,050; Length: 245.5 ft; Breadth: 61.2 ft; Depth: 25.8 ft; Draught: 26.3 ft. (mean); Speed: 11 knots; Crew: 1100; Engines: Steam, 2 cylinder return connecting rod type. 3,000 b.h.p. at 57.5 r.p.m. Boiler pressure 20 p.s.i; Screws: 1; Armament: Lower deck: 10-8 in. and 26-32 pdrs. Middle deck: 6-8 in. and 30-32 pdrs. Main deck: 38-32 pdrs. Upper deck: 20-32 pdrs. and 1-68 pdr*

GREAT EASTERN (1859): This gigantic iron hulled ship was immensely strong but very underpowered. Built before her time, she brought several firms to bankruptcy. Instead of Eastern service as intended she made 11 transatlantic voyages, but carried only a fraction of the passengers hoped for.

Short-lived success as a cable ship—mainly on the Atlantic—ended with long idleness. After two years as an exhibition ship she arrived at Birkenhead 1888 to be scrapped.

DATA: *Previous name: LEVIATHAN; Builders: Scott, Russell & Co., Millwall; Launched (sideways): 31 January 1858; Completed: September 1859; Cargo capacity: 6,000 tons; Tonnage (gross): 18,915; Length, waterline: 680 ft; Breadth: 82.7 ft. (118 ft. over paddle boxes); Depth: 58 ft; Draught: 30 ft; Speed: 11 knots (average); Crew: 400; Passengers: 800 first, 2,000 second, 1200 third; Engines: (for paddles) 1—4 cyl. oscillating type 3410 h.p. at 10.75 r.p.m; (for screw) 1—4 cyl. horizontal direct acting type; 4,890 h.p. at 38 r.p.m. 10 boilers, 25 p.s.i; Screws: One, and paddles*

MALABAR (1860): Like all Blackwall frigates, this had the outward appearance of a man-of-war—also quarter galleries, which for other types had long been discarded. The MALABAR was employed in the East Indian trade and, for a while, was a favourite trooper. She remained with her original owners until 1878 when she was bought by another London firm. Although no clipper, she was reasonably fast, and in 1867 returned from the Bay of Bengal to Dover in 89 days. Historically the Blackwall frigates were the lineal descendants of the well-found but cumbrous vessels of the East India Company. With the ending of its monopoly, the ships were sold, but were found too slow to meet growing competition. Hence the development of a new type, faster, but still able to take large cargoes.

DATA: *Owners: Green's Blackwall Line; Builders: William Pile, Sunderland; Completed: 1860; Gross Tonnage: 1,219; Length between perps: 207.2 ft; Breadth: 36.6 ft; Depth: 22.5 ft; Passengers: Certainly a few*

IMPERATRICE EUGENIE (1865): The C.G.T. commenced operations as such in 1862 with two purchased vessels. Eight large iron ships were then ordered from Scotts of Greenock, three to be built there, the others in France under Scotts' direction. The IMPERATRICE EUGENIE, the first of the latter group, was notable as the first Atlantic liner to be built in France, also as the last for that trade to have paddles. She was one of several used on the service to Central America. Her passenger capacity is not recorded, only that on one 1866 voyage she carried 600. Later lengthened, converted to screw and twice re-engined, she was wrecked as the AMERIQUE in 1895.

DATA: *Owners: Cie. Generale Transatlantique; Builders: Chantier de l'Atlantique, St. Nazaire; Launched: 23 April 1864; Entered service: 16 February 1865; Tonnage (gross): 3,200 (later 4,585); Length between perps: 355 ft. (later 394 ft.); Breadth: 44 ft; Speed: 12 knots; Engines: Side-lever type 2 cyls., 94.5 in. dia., 104 in. stroke*

ARIEL (1865) and TAEPING (1863): In the years before the opening of the Suez Canal in 1869 the annual race of the China tea clippers to London with the first of the new crop was something which aroused widespread public interest. The fastest ships earned high freights and a bonus was paid for the first cargo in. Fine lined and relatively small, these tea clippers were driven so hard that they seldom lasted long. The most famous race was that shown, which ended early in September 1866 when the ARIEL (right) and the TAEPING raced up the English Channel after having left the Min River in May. The ARIEL—claimed as the fastest and finest of them all—was dangerously slim aft, and many blamed this for her disappearance in the Indian Ocean in 1872.

DATA: *Builders: R. Steele & Co., Greenock (both ships); Completed: 1865, 1863; Tonnage (gross): 857, 767; Length between perps: 197.4, 183.7 ft; Breadth: 33.9, 31.1 ft; Depth of hold: 19.6, 19.9 ft.*

CUTTY SARK (1869): This century-old ship, now permanently preserved at Greenwich, is the only survivor of the famous China tea clippers. In fact, she was built too late for the trade which was then passing to steamers. She made eight voyages in the tea trade, but it was later as an Australian wool clipper that she really proved herself. On one occasion she overtook a crack P. & O. liner which was doing 16 knots, and for the ten year period 1885-95 she made the fastest voyages home with wool, coming via the Horn. Sold to Portugal in 1895, she was bought back in 1922 and restored. Thereafter she lay at Falmouth and Greenhithe before coming to Greenwich.

DATA: *Owners: Originally Captain John Willis, London; Builders: Scott & Linton, Dumbarton (completed by Denny); Launched: 22 November 1869; First voyage: from London 16 February 1870, to Shanghai; Tonnage (gross): 963; (displacement): 2100; Length overall: 280 ft; Length between perps: 212.5 ft; Breadth: 36 ft; Depth: 22.5 ft; Draught 20 ft.*

OCEANIC (1871): For her day this ship was of exceptionally advanced design. Historic as the first steamer to be built for the famous White Star Line, she was the lead ship of a class of four designed for the Liverpool—New York service. Among the many features which she introduced was the placing of first class accommodation amidships, away from screw vibration. As regards machinery, the adoption of compound engines was notable, likewise the advance in boiler pressure. After making 33 round Atlantic voyages, she inaugurated a new trans-Pacific service in 1875, and operated

there (on charter) with great success until 1894. She was scrapped the following year.

DATA: *Owners: Oceanic Steam Navigation Co. (White Star Line) Builders: Harland & Wolff, Belfast; Launched: 27 August 1870; Maiden voyage: 2 March 1871; Tonnage (gross): 3,707; Length between perps: 420 ft; Breadth: 40.9 ft; Depth of hold: 23.4 ft; Speed: 14 knots; Passengers: Approx. 160 first, 1,000 steerage; Engines: One 4 cyl. compound expansion, 1,990 I.h.p. 12 boilers, 65 p.s.i; Screws: 1*

H.M.S. THUNDERER (1872): This turret battleship and her sister DEVASTATION were built when the Royal Navy was breaking free from many traditions which were almost age-old. Sail had been discarded, so too old style masts and riggings, this demanding new principles for the classification of types. The DEVASTATION and THUNDERER were the first sea-going battleships to be built without rigging. Their hulls, low and very beamy, had main armament in two turrets, one forward, one aft. For the first time guns and turrets were hydraulically operated. The THUNDERER's original big muzzle loading guns were replaced by breech loaders in 1891. She was sold out of the Navy in 1909.

DATA: *Builders: Pembroke Dockyard; Launched: 25 March 1872; Tonnage (displacement): 9,390; Length between perps: 285 ft; Breadth: 62 ft. 3 ins; Draught: 27 ft. 6 ins; Speed: 14 knots; Crew: 420; Engines: 2 sets inverted triple-expansion. 7,000 i.h.p.(max); Screws: 2; Armament: 4—12 inch (later 4—10 in.), 6—6 pdrs. & smaller guns, 2 Torpedo Tubes*

TONNERRE (1875): The revolving armoured turret was developed in the 1860s, and two-turret battleships became the vogue during the decade which followed. Safety at sea in heavy weather was impaired by lack of freeboard, but this did not apply to local Defence ships.

The TONNERRE was one of 12 Coast Defence ironclads launched 1863-83 for the French Navy. She lasted well, not being scrapped until 1905. Built of iron and steel, she had both big guns (breech loaders) on a single turret. This, like the redoubt and bulkheads, was protected by 11.8 ins. of armour. Her main armour belt varied in thickness from 9.8 ins. to 12.9 ins.

DATA: *Builders: Naval Dockyard, Toulon; Launched: 1875; Tonnage (displacement): 5,589; Length: 248 ft; Breadth: 57 ft. 9 ins; Draught: 22 ft. 3 ins. (mean); Speed: 14 knots (max) 11 at sea, Crew: 228; Engines: steam, direct induction, 4,165 l.h.p. 32 boilers; Screws: One; Armament: 2–10.6 in. 4–4.7 in. guns, 6–1 pdr. revolving cannon. 2 torpedo tubes*

CLEOPATRA (1877): Before the famous Needle was erected on the Embankment on 12 September 1878, it had made a strange and hazardous voyage. First erected at Heliopolis about 1500 B.C., it spent centuries in the sand at Alexandria before being presented to Britain in 1819. Officialdom vetoed all attempts to bring it to London until 1877. A prefabricated iron cylinder 93 ft. x 15 ft. was shipped out and assembled round the obelisk, which was then rolled into the water. A boulder pierced the hull and the launch was not completed until September 7th. Once afloat, it was given bilge keels and ballast, a bridge, cabin, sails and rudder. On September 21st, the Obelisk ship was towed away by the s.s. OLGA, but during a Biscay gale it broke adrift and had to be abandoned—six being drowned in a rescue effort. Retrieved by another ship, the CLEOPATRA finally reached London on January 20th, 1878, in tow of the three funnelled tug ANGLIA

BALLAARAT (1882): Of the three main P. & O. services—to India, the Far East and Australia—the last named had become the most important when this ship was built. Instead of previous interchangeability of ships, the BALLAARAT and her sister PARRAMATTA—also brig-rigged—formed the nucleus of a special Australian fleet. Known not only for their good looks, their accommodation was regarded as luxurious. Their public rooms had particularly fine carvings, and first class cabins had iron beds, not bunks. In 1900 the BALLAARAT was used to carry troops to China. Withdrawn in 1904, she was sold to Genoese breakers and made her final voyage there with the name abbreviated to LAARAT.

DATA: *Owners: Peninsular & Oriental Steam Nav. Co; Builders: Caird & Co., Greenock; Completed: 1882; Tonnage (gross): 4752; Length between perps: 420.2 ft; Breadth: 43.0 ft; Depth: 34.5 ft; Speed: 14 knots; Passengers: Approx. 160 first, 48 second class; Engines: Steam, inverted compound, 4,300 I.h.p. 4 D.E. boilers, 90 p.s.i; Screws: One*

CONQUEROR (1884): For the propulsion of seagoing vessels, the screw duly proved its superiority over the paddle. However, for types such as excursion ships and tugs whose work entailed much manoeuvring, the paddle long remained the more popular. For turning it was much easier and quicker, while for towing—even astern—the paddles could get a useful grip on the water.

The iron hulled CONQUEROR, originally used for Thames towing and excursion work, next spent some years under the French flag before starting a long period of service on the North East Coast. When scrapped in 1956 she was the last Tyne paddle tug with two funnels abreast.

DATA: *Previous names: ex CONQUERANT ex CONQUEROR; Owners: France Fenwick Tyne & Wear Co. Ltd., Newcastle; Builders: Hepple & Co., North Shields; Completed. 1884. Gross Tonnage: 177; Length between perps: 123.5 ft; Breadth: 20.1 ft; Depth: 10.1 ft; Engines: Steam side lever engines; 2 cyls. 32 ins. dia; 58 ins. stroke; Screws: Paddle*

UMBRIA (1884): The UMBRIA and her sister ETRURIA were amongst the last Atlantic fliers to have single screws, and the very last with compound engines. Among Cunard mail ships, they were the first to have the dining saloon amidships, not aft. Used on the Liverpool—New York service, they proved outstandingly successful. They were designed for quick conversion into auxiliary cruisers, one requirement being ability to maintain 18 knots for 16 days. The performance of both these record-breakers improved with age, although excessive vibration caused shaft trouble.

UMBRIA was finally scrapped in 1910, her sister a year earlier.

DATA: *Owners: Cunard Steam Ship Co. Ltd; Builders: J. Elder & Co., Glasgow; Completed: October 1884; Tonnage (gross): 7,718 (later 8,128); Length between perps: 501.6 ft; Breadth: 57.2 ft; Depth: 40.0 ft; Speed: 19½ knots; Passengers: As built approx. 550 first, 800 steerage; Engines: Compound expansion, 3 cyls. 71 ins. dia. and (2) 105 ins. dia., 72 ins. stroke. 14,000 I.h.p; Screws: 1*

ANDREA DORIA (1885): This Italian battleship was one of three, her sisters being the FRANCESCO MOROSINI and RUGGIERO DI LAURIA. She remained on the effective list until 1911. Her four big guns (breech-loaders) were in two barbettes amidships and their barrels, dark painted and tilted, are just visible beneath the funnels. Amidships she had what was termed a military mast. By 1890 the Italian Navy ranked second in power to the British, although in terms of tonnage it came third, after France. For their size many Italian ships were unusually fast and heavily armed. Intended only for Mediterranean use, a reduced bunker capacity was justified. **DATA:** *Builders: Naval yard, Spezia; Launched: 1885; Tonnage (displacement): 11,200; Length: 328 ft. 2 ins; Breadth: 65 ft. 4 ins; Draught: 27 ft. 2 ins; Speed: 16 knots; Engines: 2 sets 3 cylinder compound expansion, 10,000 l.h.p. 8 boilers; Screws: 2; Armament: 4–17 in., 2–6 in., 4–4.7 in. guns. 5 Torpedo tubes*

GLUCKAUF (1886): Accepted as the prototype of today's giant tankers, the GLUCKAUF was the first oiler to be specially built for ocean service in which the oil was carried next the hull. Hitherto shallow draft bulk oil carriers had been used in the Volga/Caspian area, but elsewhere the use of barrels was still normal. The GLUCKAUF's cargo space was divided by a single longitudinal bulkhead and the usual transverse ones. She could unload in 12 hours. Her sister VORWARTS was lost in 1890, but the GLUCKAUF continued trading until 1893, when she stranded on Fire Island near New York.

DATA: *Owners: German-American Petroleum Co., Hamburg; Builders: Sir W.G. Armstrong Mitchell & Co., Newcastle; Launched: June 16, 1886; Completed: July 10, 1886; Tonnage (gross): 2307; (deadweight): approx. 3020; Length between perps: 300.5 ft, Breadth: 37.2 ft; Depth: 23.2 ft; Speed: 10½ knots (trials); Engines: Reciprocating Steam, Triple expansion, 900 l.h.p; 2 boilers, 150 p.s.i; Screws: One*

CITY OF PARIS (1889): The second of a pair, she and the CITY OF NEW YORK were, when new, the largest and fastest in service. They were also the first express liners with twin screws. The CITY OF PARIS, the later by eight months, made her first sailing (Liverpool—New York) in April 1889, and on her second voyage proved a record-breaker. In 1893 she was renamed PARIS and in May 1899 stranded as shown on the Manacles. Refloated, modernised and re-engined, she returned to service in 1901 as the American Line's two funnelled PHILADELPHIA. Sold in 1922, she was scrapped a year later.

DATA: *Owners: Inman & International Steamship Co; Builders: J. & G. Thomson, Clydebank; Launched: 23 October, 1888; Tonnage (gross): 10,499; (displacement): 13,000; Length overall: 560 ft; Breadth: 63.2 ft; Depth: 39.2 ft; Draught: 23 ft; Speed: 20 knots; Passengers: Nearly 2,000, in three classes; Engines: 2 sets steam triple expansion, 20,000 I.h.p; Screws: 2*

H.M.S. REVENGE (1892): For British battleship design, the ROYAL SOVEREIGN class ships marked the end of an experimental phase—and they were in fact the prototypes of the classic battleship. The seven units were ROYAL SOVEREIGN, ROYAL OAK, REVENGE, RESOLUTION, REPULSE, RAMILLIES and EMPRESS OF INDIA (ex RENOWN). Notably superior to Britain's earlier ships, they were without equal abroad. Subsequent addition of bilge keels reduced excessive rolling. Their main guns—breech loaders—were mounted in armoured barbettes 17 ins. thick.

They were hydraulically operated, but could only be loaded when in centreline position—a fault rectified in later designs. REVENGE, renamed REDOUBTABLE in 1915, was sold late 1919.

DATA: *Builders: Palmers, Jarrow; Launched: 3 November, 1892; Tonnage (displacement): 14,150; Length (waterline): 380 ft; Breadth: 75 ft; Draught: 28 ft; Speed: 17.5 knots; Crew: 710 (later 660); Engines: 2 Steam triple-expansion, 8 SE boilers. 13,000 s.h.p; Screws: 2; Armament: 4—13.5 in., 12—6 in., 16—6 pdr., 13—12 pdr. guns, 7 torpedo tubes*

ISLE OF ARRAN (1892): Before the days of motoring, a trip by paddle steamer was a "must" for holidaymakers. Fares were absurdly cheap, and for a few shillings one could spend hours afloat—with refreshments readily available in the saloons.

The Clyde had Britain's largest fleet of excursion ships, amongst them the ISLE OF ARRAN owned by Buchanan (later Williamson-Buchanan. Apart from war service—at first minesweeping and then bringing home troops from France— she operated on the Clyde from 1892 until her sale early 1933. For the next four seasons she plied on the Thames as shown, making trips to the docks, Herne Bay, and the Nore.

DATA: *Owners: General Steam Navigation Co. Ltd., London (from 1933 to 1936); Builders: T.B. Seath & Co., Rutherglen; Launched: 14 May, 1892; Tonnage (gross): 313; Length between perps: 210 ft; Breadth: 24 ft; Depth: 7.4 ft; Speed: 15 knots; Passengers: 1,300; Engines: Steam, single cylinder 52 ins. dia., 60 ins. stroke; Paddle*

BRITANNIA (1893): Built for King Edward VII, this black hulled cutter did much to revive interest in yacht racing. Her first race was on 25 May, 1893, and by winning it she set the pattern for future years. From 1899 however she was used for cruising with a sail area much reduced from its original 10,300 sq. ft. In 1913, under the ownership of King George V—whose favourite she was—she returned to handicap racing. This was resumed in 1920, but from then on she underwent many rig changes. By 1931 she had shed her gaff and become a Bermudan cutter (as shown). After the death of the King in 1936 she was taken to sea and scuttled.

DATA: *Builders: D. & W. Henderson, Partick; Launched: 1893; Tonnage (Thames Measurement): 221; (displacement): 160; Length overall: 124 ft; Length between perps: 88 ft; Breadth: 23 ft; Draught: 15 ft. 3 ins.*

TURBINIA (1894): This vessel was the first ever to be propelled by turbines. She was built in a small hired yard at Wallsend—for experimental purposes and to demonstrate the potential of the Parsons turbine. Early results with one turbine driving a single shaft were disappointing. She was then given three shafts, each shaft with its three propellers being driven by a separate, direct coupled turbine. With this greater propeller surface all went well; and at the Diamond Jubilee Naval Review held at Spithead 1897, she made a sensational order-winning display by travelling at an unprecedented 34.5 knots.

DATA: *Owners and Builders: The Parsons Marine Steam Turbine Co; Completed: 1894; Tonnage (displacement): 44.5; Length overall: 100 ft; Breadth: 9 ft; Depth: 7 ft; Draught: 3 ft; Speed: 34.5 knots; Engines: Originally one, later three Parsons steam turbines 2,000 s.h.p. 1 Yarrow D.E. Watertube boiler, 210 p.s.i; Screws: Originally 1. From 1896 3*

KAISER WILHELM DER GROSSE (1897): Built for the express service between Bremerhaven, Southampton and New York. For two years she was the world's largest liner. Late in 1897 she became Germany's first Blue Riband holder; on the Eastwards run she averaged 22.35 knots. She was consistently fast, but KAISER FRIEDRICH—her intended opposite number—so lacked speed that the N.D.L. refused acceptance.

In 1900 the WILHELM was one of the first to be given radio—its range 25 miles. The year 1913 saw her downgraded to carry third class and steerage only. While acting as an Armed Merchant Cruiser she was sunk off West Africa on 27 August, 1914, by H.M.S. HIGHFLYER.

DATA: *Owners: Norddeutscher Lloyd, Bremen; Builders: A.G. Vulcan, Stettin; Launched: 4 May, 1897; Maiden voyage: September 1897; Tonnage (gross): 14,349; (displacement): 20,000; Length overall: 648.6 ft; Breadth: 66 ft; Depth: 43 ft; Speed: 22 knots; Passengers: 332/343/1074; Engines: 2 sets 4 cyl. triple expansion, 28,000 l.h.p. 15 boilers; Screws: 2*

MINTO (1898): This wood-burning stern-wheeler was intended for the Klondyke gold rush traffic on the Stikine River. Built in 1,000 pieces, these were sent by train across Canada for assembly at Vancouver. Arriving too late for that project, they were then railed to Nakusp, B.C., on the Arrow Lakes, and there put together.

On them she plied between Arrowhead and West Robson—a 12 hour trip—and besides serving various settlements en route, she would also stop in response to a signal fire or flag from a hunter or logger wanting to embark. The MINTO travelled 2½ million miles before being withdrawn in 1954. Later sold for scrap, her remains were burned in 1968.

DATA: *Owners: Canadian Pacific Rly. Co., Montreal; Builders: Bertram Iron Works, Toronto (for reassembly); Launched: 1898 at Nakusp; Tonnage (gross): 829; Length between perps: 162 ft; Breadth: 30 ft; Depth: 6 ft; Speed: 12—13 knots; Passengers: 225; Engines: Steam compound horizontal, driving stern wheel*

OCEANIC (1899): The largest liner of the 19th century, the OCEANIC was built for the Liverpool—New York service, but from 1907 was based on Southampton. Her slim hull (length ten times the beam) vibrated badly at full speed. Less speedy than anticipated, she became famed instead for her steadiness and luxury. She was wrecked on Foula Island in the Shetlands, September 1919, just after being requisitioned as an Armed Merchant Cruiser.

DATA: *Owners: Oceanic Steam Navigation Co. (White Star Line); Builders: Harland & Wolff, Belfast; Launched: 14 January, 1899; Maiden voyage: 6 September, 1899; Tonnage (gross): 17,274; (displacement): 28,000; Length overall: 704.0 ft; Length between perps: 685.7 ft; Breadth: 68.4 ft; Depth: 49 ft; Speed: 19 knots; Crew: 390; Passengers: 1,700 in first, second and third classes; Engines: Two 4 cyl. triple expansion, 28,000 l.h.p. 12 D.E. and 3 S.E. boilers 192 p.s.i; Screws: 2*

H.M.S. CRESSY (1899): The name ship of a class of six armoured cruisers, the others being the SUTLEJ, ABOUKIR, HOGUE, BACCHANTE, and EURYALUS. All gave long and useful service in foreign stations, but by the start of World War I they were becoming worn out. The ABOUKIR was torpedoed by U9 in the North Sea on 22nd September, 1914, and while closing to pick up survivors, CRESSY and HOGUE were also sunk. The CRESSY's were the first of seven classes of armoured cruisers built 1901-08, all four funnelled but varying between 9,800 and 16,100 tons. Their conning towers' armour was 12 ins. thick, the main belt being 6 ins. **DATA**: *Builders: Fairfield, Glasgow; Launched: 4 December, 1899; Completed: 1901; Tonnage (displacement): 12,000; Length (waterline): 454 ft; Breadth: 69 ft. 6 ins; Draught: 28 ft; Speed: 20 knots; Crew: 700+; Engines: 2 sets of 4 cylinder triple expansion, 21,000 l.h.p. 31 boilers; Screws: 2; Armament: 2—9.2 in., 12—6 in., 13—12 pdr. and smaller guns, 2—18 in. torpedo tubes*

H.M.S. ARAB (1901): Early destroyers like the ARAB had low hulls and despite the turtleback were very wet at sea. This was cured on the RIVER class (1903) which were the first with a raised forecastle.

The ARAB, the sixth of her name in the Royal Navy, was one of the "30 knot class" of which 23 were built 1896-1903. Their builders had much latitude, so appearance varied, also number of funnels. The choice of machinery resulted from an earlier accident which had somewhat shaken official faith in turbines. The ARAB spent her whole career in home waters and was scrapped in 1919.

DATA: *Builders: J. & G. Thomson, Clydebank; Launched: 9 February, 1901; Tonnage (displacement): 470; Length overall: 227.5 ft; Breadth: 22.3ft; Depth: 9.8 ft; Draught: 5 ft. (mean); Speed: 31 knots; Crew: 60; Engines: Two sets steam triple expansion, 8,600 h.p. Normand boilers. Coal 90 tons; Screws: 2; Armament: 1—12 pdr. (forward), 5—6 pdr. guns, 2—18 in. torpedo tubes*

H.M. "SUBMARINE NO. 2" (1902): The Admiralty ordered its first submarines (Nos. 1–5) from Vickers, Barrow, in 1900, and these were completed in 1902–3. Known as the HOLLAND class—after the American designer A.P. Holland—they had single hulls, internal ballast tanks and a bow torpedo tube. These five were purely experimental, and provided much useful experience before being sold. Nos. 1 and 2 were the last to go, in 1913. Britain's first operational submarines, the A class, followed in 1903-4.

These were 100 ft. long and introduced the conning tower. Thereafter progress was rapid.

DATA: *Builders: Vickers, Barrow; Completed: 1902; Tonnage (displacement): 104 tons surface, 150 tons submerged; Length overall: 63 ft. 4 ins; Breadth: 11 ft. 9 ins; Speed: 8 knots (surface), 5 knots submerged; Crew: 7; Engines: One petrol motor, 250 h.p., for surface use, battery driven electric motor when submerged; Screws: One; Armament: One—14 in. Torpedo Tube*

ARMADALE CASTLE (1903): This was the first Mail ship to be built for the Union-Castle Line following its creation in 1900 out of the amalgamation of two long-term rival concerns. She and her sister KENILWORTH CASTLE were the largest on the Cape run until joined in 1910 by the similar looking BALMORAL CASTLE and EDINBURGH CASTLE. As mail ships, they then sailed from Southampton every Saturday with a Tuesday-week dawn arrival at the other end. During the 1914-18 war the ARMADALE CASTLE served as an Auxiliary Cruiser. She resumed commercial service in 1919, continuing until 1936 when she was scrapped.

DATA: *Owners: The Union-Castle Mail S.S. Co. Ltd; Builders: Fairfield Co. Ltd., Glasgow; Launched: 11 August, 1903; Tonnage (gross): 12,973; (deadweight): 10,300; Length between perps: 570.1 ft; Breadth: 64.5 ft; Depth: 42.5 ft; Speed: 17 knots; Passengers: 260 first, 300 second class; Engines: 2 sets steam quadruple expansion. 6 D.E. and 4 S.E. boilers, 220 p.s.i; Screws: 2*

THE QUEEN (1903): This was the world's first turbine-driven cross channel ship. Her immediate success on the Dover—Calais route led to the construction of four sisters, the ONWARD and INVICTA in 1905 and the EMPRESS and VICTORIA in 1907. Of their turbines, the H.P. unit drove the centre shaft, the L.P. ones the wing shafts—which could also go astern.

THE QUEEN and ONWARD survived a fog collision in 1908, and in the autumn of 1914 the former rescued 2,200 persons from the torpedoed French liner AMIRAL GANTEAUME. She herself was sunk by torpedo on 26 August, 1916.

DATA: *Owners: South Eastern & Chatham Railway Co; Builders: Wm. Denny & Bros., Dumbarton; Completed: 1903; Tonnage (gross): 1,676; Length between perps: 309.9 ft; Breadth: 40 ft; Depth of hold: 15 ft. 7 ins; Speed: 21¾ knots; Passengers: Approx. 1,250; Engines: Three steam turbines, direct drive; Screws: Three*

H.M.S. BRITANNIA (1906): The seventh unit of the KING EDWARD VII class battleships, the others being the COMMONWEALTH, DOMINION, HINDUSTAN, ZEALANDIA, HIBERNIA and AFRICA. They were the last to be designed by Sir William White, and thus the last of many with this style profile. A new feature was the inclusion of 9.2 in. guns (visible by masts) these supplementing ten 6 in. guns (visible on deck below). New appearance changes were the substitution of a gun control position for the former fighting tops and the elimination of an after bridge. The

BRITANNIA was sunk by U.B.50 off Cape Trafalgar in November 1918.

DATA: *Builders: H.M. Dockyard, Portsmouth; Launched: 10 December, 1904; Completed: 1906; Tonnage (displacement): 16,350; Length waterline: 439 ft; Breadth: 78 ft; Draught: 26 ft. 9 ins; Speed: 18 knots; Crew: about 800; Engines: 2 sets steam triple expansion, 18,000 l.h.p; Screws: Two; Armament: 4—12 in., 4—9.2 in., 10—6 in., 13—12 pdr. and 17 smaller guns, 4 or 5—18 in. torpedo tubes*

H.M.S. DREADNOUGHT (1906): By mounting more big guns and of a greater size, and having a like superiority in speed, this battleship made all previous ones obsolete. Six of her guns could fire forward, six aft and eight on the beam. One defect was the placing of a funnel forward of the mast, for the gun control could be made untenable by smoke. Her protective armour was up to 11 ins. thick. In the North Sea, March 1915, she succeeded in ramming and sinking a German submarine – the U 29 – whose Captain had previously torpedoed the cruisers CRESSY (q.v.) HOGUE, ABOUKIR, and HAWKE. The DREADNOUGHT was scrapped 1923.

DATA: *Builders: R.N. Dockyard, Portsmouth; Launched: 10 February, 1906; Completed: October 1906; Tonnage (full load displacement): 22,200; Length (waterline): 520 ft; Breadth: 82 ft; Draught: 31 ft; Speed: 21 knots; Crew: About 750; Engines: Parsons turbines, direct drive, 23,000 s.h.p., 18 boilers; Screws: 4; Armament: 10–12 in., 24–12 pdr. guns, 5 Torpedo Tubes*

CLAN BUCHANAN (1907): The turret steamer was designed by Doxford's in the early 'nineties, and many were built during the next 20 years. As a general cargo carrier it had two strong sales points. With its novel shape and narrow top (turret) deck, the hull was immensely strong—yet the weight of framing was less than usual. This saving in weight raised cargo capacity. Also, as regulations then stood, the space above the narrow "harbour decks" (where width decreased) was exempted from tonnage calculations, so cutting harbour dues. The last of 30 turret ships built for the Clan Line, the

CLAN BUCHANAN continued trading until the early thirties.

DATA: *Owners: Cayzer Irvine & Co. (Clan Line), London; Builders: Wm. Doxford & Sons, Sunderland; Launched: 24 September, 1907; Tonnage (gross): 5,212; (deadweight): 8,150; Length between perps: 400.1 ft; Breadth: 52.1 ft; Depth of hold: 27.4 ft; Draught: 25 ft. 2 ins; Speed: 12 knots; Engines: Steam, triple expansion, coal fired boilers; Screws: One*

MAURETANIA (1907): The first express liners to be turbine driven, the MAURETANIA and her Clyde-built sister LUSITANIA were the largest and fastest yet built. Slightly the better performer, the MAURETANIA averaged 25.04 knots on trial. Her speed improved with age, and she retained the Blue Riband until 1929. Losing it to the BREMEN, she then did her best ever, crossing East and West at 26.85 and 27.22 knots respectively, with an up-channel burst of 29.7 knots. Used from 1931 as a cruise ship, she was scrapped in 1935.

DATA: *Owners: Cunard Steam Ship Co. Ltd; Builders: Swan, Hunter & Wigham Richardson, Newcastle; Launched: 20 September, 1906; Maiden voyage: 16 November, 1907; Tonnage (gross): 31,938; (displacement): 43,000; Length between perps: 762.2 ft; Breadth: 88 ft; Depth: 60.5 ft; Draught: 25 ft. 1 in; Speed: 25 knots; Crew: 1266 (original figure); Passengers: 563/464/1,138 (original figures); Engines: 4 Steam turbines, 68,000 s.h.p; 35 boilers, 195 p.s.i; Screws: 4*

DRESDEN (1909): All German light cruisers operating during the first World War had town names. The DRESDEN and EMDEN were sisters, although the latter had twin screws and reciprocating engines. Each had a single 4.1 in. gun forward and aft, the rest being on the beam. Shape of stem gave indication of age. The oldest light cruisers had very extended ram bows, the final ones stems (straight or curved) which sloped in the opposite direction.

After some commerce raiding in the South Atlantic, she was the only German warship to escape from the Battle of the Falklands. Thereafter chased, she was scuttled at Juan Fernandez March 1915 to avoid capture.

DATA: *Builders: Blohm & Voss, Hamburg; Launched: October 1907; Completed: 1909; Tonnage (displacement): 3,600; Length overall: 395 ft; Breadth: 43 ft. 4 ins; Draught: 17 ft. 9 ins; Speed: 24.5 knots; Crew: Around 350; Engines: Parsons geared turbines, 15,000 h.p. (trials), 12 boilers; Screws: Four; Armament: 10—4.1 in., 8—5 pdr. guns, 2—17.7 in. Torpedo Tubes (submerged)*

NELEUS (1911): Alfred Holt's Blue Funnel Line has always been known for the high quality of its ships, and the NELEUS was one of nine similar cargo liners built for them 1908-11. She had four main holds and was of the familiar three island type, i.e. with raised forecastle, bridge deck and poop. Amidships she had a limited amount of first class accommodation. When required she could carry steerage passengers in the forecastle, and native passengers aft. A coal burner, she had bunker space for 1,100 tons and used about 75 tons per day. She gave long service and it was not until late 1948 that she was sold for scrap.

DATA: *Owners: China Mutual Steam Nav. Co., (Alfred Holt & Co.), Liverpool; Builders: Workman Clark & Co., Belfast; Launched: 31 January, 1911; Tonnage (gross): 6,685; (deadweight): 8,500; Length overall: 457 ft; Breadth: 52 ft; Depth of hold: 32 ft; Speed: 13–14 knots; Engines: Steam, triple expansion, 2 D.E. boilers; Screws: One*

VERGNIAUD (1911): This French battleship was one of the DANTON class, all six of which were completed in 1913. Numerous funnels, of strange shape and often in widely separated groups, were long a characteristic of French warships. These were the only battleships to have five funnels, but several of their cruisers had six. The DANTONs had their main guns paired on the centreline, their secondary (9.2 in.) guns being also paired, six on each broadside. The main armour belt was 10 ins. thick. Of this class, only the

DANTON was sunk—near Sicily in 1917. The VERGNIAUD was removed from the effective list in 1921.

DATA: *Builders: Chantiers de la Gironde, Bordeaux; Completed: September 1911; Tonnage (displacement): 18,400; Length (waterline): 475 ft. 9 ins; Breadth: 84 ft. 9 ins; Draught: 27 ft. 6 ins; Speed: 19½ knots; Crew: 680; Engines: Parsons Steam turbines, 22,500 s.h.p; Screws: 4; Armament: 4–12 in., 12–9.4 in., 14–12 pdr. and 10 smaller guns. 2–18 in. torpedo tubes*

72

TITANIC (1912): The world's largest liner, she left Southampton on 10 April 1912 on her maiden voyage for Queenstown (Cobh) and New York.

Four days later, at 11.40 p.m., she collided with an iceberg. For this, and her subsequent loss, the British Court of Inquiry blamed "the excessive speed at which she was being navigated". Torn open for some 300 ft., low on the starboard side, she sank vertically, bow first, disappearing from sight at 2.20 a.m.

DATA: *Owners: Oceanic Steam Navigation Co. (White Star Line); Builders: Harland & Wolff, Belfast; Launched: 31 May, 1911; Tonnage (gross): 46,329; (displacement): 52,250; Length overall: 882.7 ft; Breadth: 92.5 ft; Depth: 59.5 ft; Draught: 34.5 ft; Speed: 21 knots; Crew: 885 (212 saved); Passengers: 325/285/706 (203/118/178 saved, official figures); Engines: Two 4 cyl. triple expansion, each 15,000 l.h.p. Turbine on centre shaft, 16,000 s.h.p. 29 Boilers; Screws: 3*

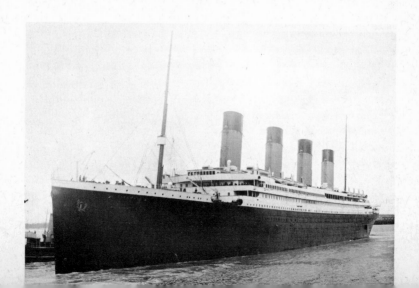

SELANDIA (1912): One of the most famous ships of the century, the SELANDIA was the world's first ocean-going motorship. She was designed for an exceptionally long route, between Copenhagen and Bangkok, yet hitherto the diesel engine had only been applied to much smaller vessels, mainly for coastal service or on inland waterways.

Despite the sceptics' pronouncements that her machinery would prove unreliable and soon wear out, the SELANDIA was so successful that her owners ceased building steamers. She remained with them until 1936. Then sold to Norway, she traded first as the NORSEMAN, next as the Finnish TORNATOR, before being wrecked off the Japanese Coast in 1942.

DATA: *Owners: East Asiatic Co., Copenhagen; Builders: Burmeister & Wain, Copenhagen; Delivered: 17 February, 1912; Tonnage (gross): 4,964; (deadweight): 7,400; Length between perps: 370.4 ft; Breadth: 53.2 ft; Depth: 30.0 ft; Speed: 10½-11 knots; Passengers: 26; Engines: Two 8 cyl. 4 stroke S.A. B. & W. diesels, 2500 l.h.p. 140 r.p.m; Screws: 2*

AQUITANIA (1914): This outstandingly successful Cunarder was designed to operate with the smaller and faster LUSITANIA and MAURETANIA on the express North Atlantic service. In essence she was a refined version of the White Star OLYMPIC/TITANIC design. Appreciably faster, she was also larger—despite tonnage similarity.

Her main period of commercial service started in 1919, when she made the first Cunard (post war) advertised voyage on the Southampton—New York route. On this she operated mainly with the MAURETANIA and BERENGARIA. The period 1939-48 was spent trooping. After two years of austerity service to Canada, she was scrapped in 1950.

DATA: *Owners: Cunard Steam Ship Co. Ltd; Builders: John Brown & Co; Launched: 21 April 1913; Maiden voyage: 30 May, 1914; Tonnage (gross): 45,647; Length overall: 901.5 ft; Length between perps: 865 ft; Breadth: 97 ft; Depth: 64.5 ft; Draught: 35.3 ft; Speed: 23 knots; Crew: 972; Passengers: 618/614/1,998; Engines: Steam turbines 56,000 s.h.p; Screws: 4*

SCOTIA II (1915): Most modern ferries have a massive superstructure above the car/train deck, but in many early ones this was not so, the hull having only the bare minimum above. This veteran was built to provide a through rail link from the Nova Scotian mainland to Cape Breton Island, carrying rolling stock across the narrow Strait of Canso. To enable her to smash her way through the thick winter ice she was given a ram bow and hull plating nearly an inch thick. A bow loader, she is unusual in having twin screws forward and

only one aft.

DATA: *Owners: Government of Canada; Builders: W.G. Armstrong Whitworth & Co., Newcastle; Launched: 13 April, 1915; Completed: August, 1915; Tonnage (gross): 1,858; (displacement): 3,665; Length overall: 300 ft; Breadth: 50 ft; Depth: 20 ft; Draught: 12 ft. 6 ins; Speed: 12 knots; Passengers: 239; Engines: 2 sets of steam triple expansion, 3,000 l.h.p. 4 Boilers; Screws: 3*

H.M.S. REPULSE (1916): Sistership RENOWN. As battlecruisers they relied on gunpower and high speed—at the expense of adequate protection. Jutland showing the weakness of the type, their most vital parts were given some more protection. Even to the end their side armour—9 ins. maximum—was too light. Used for several Royal tours, the REPULSE was reconstructed 1932-36.

In World War II she did much convoy escort work, in the North and South Atlantic. With the battleship PRINCE OF WALES she was sunk off Malaya 1941 by Japanese aerial torpedoes.

DATA: *Builders: J. Brown, Clydebank; Launched: 8 January, 1916; Completed: August 1916; Tonnage (full load displacement): 36,800; Length overall: 794 ft; Breadth: 102 ft. 8 ins. (over bulges); Draught: 31 ft. 9 ins; Speed: 29 knots (max over 31); Crew: 1200; Engines: Brown Curtis turbines 112,000 s.h.p. 42 Boilers; Screws: 4; Armament: 6—15 in., 12—4 in., 8—4 in. 4A., 4—3 pdr. guns and smaller. 8 Torpedo tubes (deck) 4 Aircraft*

ORANGELEAF (1917): This fast tanker, a Royal Fleet Auxiliary, was one of a class of six launched 1917—the others being the APPLELEAF, BRAMBLELEAF, CHERRYLEAF, PEARLEAF and PLUMLEAF. They were designed to carry U.S. oil to Britain and at the same time act as escorts to Atlantic convoys. America then being neutral, they were managed by a commercial firm, Lane & Macandrew.

Their cargo capacity was about 5,400 tons. In peacetime, when they might be on charter, they operated at about 12

knots—since at full speed fuel consumption was very high, over 90 tons per day. The ORANGELEAF was broken up in 1946.

DATA: *Owners: The Admiralty; Builders: J.L. Thompson & Sons, Sunderland; Launched: 1917; Tonnage (gross): 5,927; Length between perps: 405 ft; Breadth: 54.5 ft; Depth: 35.2 ft; Draught: 27 ft. 6 ins; Speed: 14 knots; Engines: 2 sets steam triple expansion, 6,750 l.h.p. 6 boilers, 200 p.s.i., oil fired; Screws: 2*

78

H.M.S. PEGASUS (1917): One of the earliest of the world's aircraft carriers, the PEGASUS was intended for the Great Eastern Railway's Harwich—Continental passenger service. In February 1917, while still on the stocks, she was bought by the Admiralty and completed as a seaplane carrier. She was one of eight cross channel or similar type ships converted for this work, their high speed making them suitable for fleet use. Main features were the large hangar aft (served by two cranes) and the forward flight deck. There the planes were handled by two derricks mounted on the twin foremast. The PEGASUS, later demoted to seaplane tender, was scrapped at Morecambe in 1931.

DATA: *Previous name: STOCKHOLM; Builders: John Brown & Co., Clydebank Launched: 9 June, 1917: Tonnage (displacement): 3,070; Length overall: 332 ft; Breadth: 43 ft; Draught: 15.6 ft; Speed: 20¼ knots; Crew: 180; Engines: Brown-Curtis geared turbines, 9,500 s.h.p; Screws: 2; Armament: 2—12 pdr. and 2—12 pdr. AA guns. 14 smaller*

WAR RULER (1919): Apart from fishing craft, nearly 2,500 British merchant ships were sunk by the enemy during the 1914-18 war. By the winter of 1916-17 the position had become so grave that urgent action was needed. The Government building programme then initiated was for ships of simple design with hulls and machinery standardised for ease of construction. Most numerous were the 400 ft. A and B type ships which differed internally in having one and two decks respectively. Austerely finished, they often had hinged stump masts with a light signal one amidships. The WAR RULER (A type) is shown on trials, camouflaged. She had a long career lasting 40 years.

DATA: *Owners: The Shipping Controller, London (British Government); Builders: Vickers Ltd., Barrow; Completed: May 1919; Tonnage (gross): 5,175; (deadweight): 8,175; Length between perps: 400 ft; Breadth: 52.4 ft; Depth: 31 ft; Draught: 25 ft. 3 ins; Speed: 11 knots; Engines: Steam, triple expansion, 2,500 l.h.p. 3 boilers, 180 p.s.i. coal fired; Screws: One*

H.M.S. HOOD (1920): One of four battlecruisers laid down in 1916, she alone was completed. Unequalled for size, "the Mighty Hood" became regarded as the symbol of British Naval supremacy. After the lessons of the Jutland battle, she was given 5,000 tons of extra protection, but this weakness was never completely rectified. In 1940 "Force H", of which she was flagship, had to destroy the French Fleet at Oran—to prevent it falling into enemy hands. On May 24, 1941, while chasing the BISMARCK (sunk three days later) the HOOD was hit by a salvo and blew up, only three surviving.

DATA: *Builders: John Brown & Co., Clydebank; Completed: 5 March, 1920; Tonnage (full load displacement): 46,200; Length overall: 860.7 ft; Breadth: 105.2 ft; Draught: 31.5 ft; Speed: 31 knots; Crew: 1400; Engines: Brown-Curtis geared turbines, 144,000 s.h.p. 24 boilers; Screws: 4; Armament: 8—15 in., 12—5.5 in., 4—4 in. A.A. & 9 smaller guns. 6 torpedo tubes*

HERTFORD (1920): As a type, the foodship fitted to carry chilled and frozen meat, dairy produce and fruit, has an importance all if its own. The HERTFORD, well known on the Australian trade, had over 450,000 cu. ft. of refrigerated space. One of those surrendered after World War I, her early background was remarkable. Ordered in 1912 as the Hamburg-Amerika Line's FRIESLAND, her design was recast in 1913 from freighter to 19,000 ton passenger ship. Then the original idea was re-adopted. Launched however as the RHEINLAND, she was renamed FRIESLAND in 1919.

Surrendered on completion, she joined the Federal Line in 1921, and remained with them until torpedoed in March 1942.

DATA: *Owners: Federal Steam Navigation Co., London; Builders: Bremer Vulkan, Vegesack; Launched: 1917; Completed: July 1920; Tonnage (gross): 10,923 (finally 11,785); (deadweight): 15,173; Length overall: 533 ft; Breadth: 64.2 ft; Depth: 41.3 ft; Draught: 31 ft. 10 ins; Speed: 13, later 14 knots; Engines: Steam triple expansion, 5 boilers (Bauer Wach exhaust turbine added later); Screws: 2*

WINDSOR CASTLE (1922): Launched by the Prince of Wales, and the first Union-Castle liner to come from Clydebank. She and her Belfast-built sister ARUNDEL CASTLE (1921) were the last liners to be given four funnels. New style "Toplis" gravity davits handled twelve of the lifeboats.

A later mail contract called for higher speed, so in 1936-7 both ships were re-engined and lengthened forward, their appearance being greatly improved by two large funnels and raked stem. The WINDSOR CASTLE was lost by aerial torpedo March 1943, when 110 miles n.w. of Algiers.

DATA: *Owners: Union-Castle Mail S.S. Co; Builders: John Brown & Co., Clydebank; Launched: 9 March 1921; Completed: March 1922; Tonnage (gross): 18,967 (later 19,141); Length between perps: 632.4 ft. (later 661.3 ft.); Breadth: 72.5 ft; Speed: 16 knots, later 19 (21 max); Crew: Approx 400; Passengers: Originally 234/302/274; Engines: S.R. geared turbines (output doubled 1937) coal, later oil fired; Screws: 2*

84

WERNER VINNEN (1922): In Germany, after the 1914-18 war, there was urgent need for ships and many strange conversions resulted. Attempting to get the best of both worlds, Vinnens built several large steel hulled auxiliary sailing ships. The WERNER VINNEN was one of five given a five-masted schooner rig, with the unusual addition of square sails on both the mizzen and fore masts. Her auxiliary diesel was one of those which had been designed for use in pairs in German submarines.

In 1937 she was rebuilt as a full powered, conventional looking motorship, needing a crew of only 20. Her career as such was brief, for she was sunk during the Second World War.

DATA: *Owners: F. A. Vinnen & Co., Bremen; Builders: Fried Krupp Akt. Ges., Kiel; Completed: 1922; Tonnage (gross): 1,859 (later 2,342); (deadweight): finally 2,500; Length between perps: 261.5 ft. (later 305.5); Breadth: 44.4 ft; Depth: 19.2 ft; Engines: One 4 cyl. S.A. 4 stroke Krupp diesel replaced 1937 by larger (930 h.p.) 6 cyl. unit of similar make; Screws: One*

FRANCONIA (1923): In the early 'twenties Cunard build 13 ships to replace war losses. These included five handsome 20,000 ton intermediate liners, the SCYTHIA, SAMARIA, LACONIA, FRANCONIA and CARINTHIA. The last named became famed for her long distance cruises. The FRANCONIA made some too, but apart from this and two charter periods 1931-32 on the New York—Bermuda run, she mainly sailed between Liverpool and New York—this up to 1939. Her accommodation was later regraded; first to cabin, second to tourist. Finally she carried 250 first, and 600 tourist class. She was sold for scrap in 1956.

DATA: *Owners: Cunard Steam Ship Co. Ltd; Builders: John Brown & Co., Clydebank; Launched: 21 October, 1922; Completed: June 1923; Tonnage (gross): 20,175; Length overall: 623.7 ft; Breadth: 73.7 ft; Depth: 53.5 ft; Draught: 31 ft. 4 ins; Speed: 16 knots; Crew: 414; Passengers: 212/356/1,266 third (as built); Engines: D.R. geared turbines, 12,500 s.h.p. 6 boilers; Screws: 2*

AORANGI (1924): One of the great pioneers in motor shipping she was, when new, the world's largest and fastest motorship, the first with four screws and the first top-flight passenger liner to be diesel driven. From 1931 she was owned by the Canadian-Australasian Line, in which the Union Line and C.P.R. each had a half share. Built for the Vancouver—Sydney trade, she first operated with the older NIAGARA (sunk 1940). After war service she returned to her old route, operating alone until 1953, when she was sold for scrap.

DATA: *Owners: Union S.S. Co. of New Zealand Ltd., Wellington; Builders: Fairfield, Glasgow; Launched: 17 June, 1924; Completed: December 1924; Tonnage (gross): 17,491; (displacement): 23,000; Length overall: 600 ft; Breadth: 72.2 ft; Depth: 46.6 ft; Draught: 27 ft. 10 ins; Speed: 16½-17 knots; Crew: 330; Passengers: Approx. 440/300/230; Engines: Four—6 cyl. 2 stroke S.A. Sulzer type diesels, 14,000 b.h.p., 135 r.p.m; Screws: 4*

BUCKAU (converted 1924): Built as a conventional three-masted auxiliary schooner, this vessel was fitted with Flettner rotors in 1924, and on early trials did well. Only 45 h.p. was needed to revolve the rotors at up to 100 r.p.m. Wind, it was claimed, blowing on these rotors (each 50 ft. x 12 ft.) created far more power than on suitably trimmed sails, thrust depending on direction and speed of rotation. Due to the variable nature of winds in European waters the idea proved impracticable. Although the larger BARBARA was built in 1926 with three rotors, she too was soon converted into a purely screw ship.

DATA: *Owners: Hanseatische Motorschiffahrt A.G., Hamburg; Builders: Fried Krupp A.G., Kiel; Completed: 1920 (as auxiliary schooner); Tonnage (gross): 497 (previously 455); Length between perps: 155.8 ft; Breadth: 29.6 ft; Depth of hold: 12.5 ft; Speed: 8 knots; Engines: One 2 cyl. 45 h.p. Krupp diesel driving 2 electric motors, one for each rotor. (One 6 cyl. M.A.N. diesel 300 b.h.p. retained for screw); Screws: One*

OTRANTO (1925): One of five 20,000 ton passenger and mail ships built 1924-29 for the Orient Line's Tilbury—Australia service, the others being the ORAMA, ORONSAY, ORFORD and ORONTES. Off season the OTRANTO frequently went cruising. In 1936 her third class accommodation was converted into tourist.

With the war she became a troopship and helped in the evacuation from France. Next fitted out as an assault ship, she took part in the North Africa, Sicily and Salerno landings. During her postwar career—which lasted until 1957—she carried tourist class only, her capacity being 1,412 passengers.

DATA: *Owners: Orient Steam Navigation Co. Ltd., London; Builders: Vickers Ltd., Barrow; Launched: 9 June, 1925; Completed: December 1925; Tonnage (gross): 20,032; Length overall: 658 ft; Breadth: 75.2 ft; Depth: 47.0 ft; Draught: 29 ft. 7 ins; Speed: 18 knots (service); Crew: Around 470; Passengers: 572 first, 1,114 Tourist class (as built); Engines: Parsons S.R. geared turbines, 20,000 s.h.p. 10 boilers, 215 p.s.i; Screws: 2*

GRIPSHOLM (1925): Previously owners of cargo ships only, the Brostrom Group of Gothenburg started a passenger service to New York in 1915. Some years elapsed before it could build to its own requirements, the outcome being the GRIPSHOLM—famous as the first North Atlantic motor liner. Outstandingly successful, she made wartime news through her International "Mercy Voyages" for the exchange of Allied/Axis Nationals. She remained with the S.A.L. until early 1954. Then sold and modernised, she re-opened the North German Lloyd's passenger service to New York. Soon renamed BERLIN, she sailed for them until 1966.

DATA: *Owners: Swedish American Line; Builders: Armstrong Whitworth & Co., Newcastle; Completed: November 1925; Tonnage (gross): 17,716; (displacement): 23,000; Length overall: 574.5 ft; Breadth: 74.4 ft; Depth: 42.5 ft; Draught: 29 ft; Speed: 17 knots; Crew: 320; Passengers: 590 first, 350 second, 1,000 third; Engines: Two Burmeister & Wain 6 cylinder 4 stroke D.A. diesels 13,500 b.h.p; Screws: 2*

ASTURIAS (1926): Briefly the world's largest motor liner, she and the ALCANTARA (1927) were designed for the South American trade. Although luxuriously appointed, initially their speed was disappointing and engine vibration bad; so in 1934-5 they were re-engined and lengthened. From then on, with turbines of greater power (and funnels raised by 15 ft.) they proved most successful. Wartime, the ASTURIAS—with one funnel and mast removed—served as a troopship, but was long out of commission following 1943 torpedo damage. Later sold to the Government, she was used to carry troops and migrants until sold for scrap in 1957.

DATA: *Owners: Royal Mail Steam Packet Co; Builders: Harland & Wolff, Belfast; Launched: 7 July, 1925; Maiden voyage: 26 February, 1926; Tonnage (gross): 22,071 (as built); Length overall: 656 ft., later 666 ft; Breadth: 78.5 ft; Depth: 44.7 ft; Speed: 16, later 18 knots; Passengers: 400/200/475; Engines: 2–8 cyl. Harland—B & W diesels, 15,000 b.h.p. later S.R. geared turbines, 20,000 s.h.p; Screws: 2*

H.M.S. NELSON (1927): The NELSON and RODNEY were Britain's most powerful battleships ever, and the only ones in the Royal Navy to have 16-inch guns. These were mounted in three triple turrets. Their shells weighed 2,461 lbs., almost three times as heavy as anything the DREADNOUGHT could have fired. Underwater protection was very good, while armour protection consisted of a 14 in. belt with 6¼ in. deck armour.

The NELSON gave excellent service during the war but was twice damaged, once by mine and once by aerial torpedo. After a final ten years as a training battleship she was scrapped at Inverkeithing in 1949.

DATA: *Builders: W.G. Armstrong Whitworth & Co., Walker; Launched: 3 September, 1927; Completed: June 1927; Tonnage (full load displacement): 33,950; Length overall: 710 ft; Breadth: 106 ft; Draught: 30 ft. (mean); Speed: 23½ knots; Crew: 1360 (war); Engines: Brown-Curtis geared turbines, 45,000 s.h.p. 8 boilers; Screws: 2; Armament: 9—16 in., 12—6 in., 6—4.7 in. and A.A. guns. 2—24.5 in. torpedo tubes*

ALNWICK (1928): Long an essential part of Britain's communications system, the coastal passenger liner was killed by the motor coach. The crack Tyne-Tees ships, the HADRIAN and BERNICIA, made the London–Newcastle run in 25 hours. In 1932 their place was taken by the smaller ALNWICK, formerly used on the Newcastle–Antwerp route. A few years later the service was made cargo only, the ALNWICK being sold to Fred Olsen. As the BALI she operated between Oslo and Rotterdam and, after the war, between Oslo and Newcastle. Replaced in 1952, she was sold to Burma, to be wrecked three years later.

DATA: *Owners: Tyne-Tees Steam Shipping Co., Newcastle; Builders: Swan, Hunter & Wigham Richardson, Newcastle; Completed: April 1928; Tonnage (gross): 1,383; (deadweight): 1,488; Length between perps: 254 ft; Breadth: 38.7 ft; Draught: 16 ft. 3 ins; Speed: 13 knots; Passengers: 71 first, 50 second class; Engines: Steam, triple expansion. 3 boilers, coal fired; Screws: One*

ULSTER MONARCH (1929): This ship made maritime history as the first fast high class cross channel vessel to be diesel driven. With the ULSTER PRINCE and ULSTER QUEEN, both delivered early 1930, she was designed for the Liverpool—Belfast service—then advertised as the Ulster Imperial Line. Since this involved a night crossing, the three had very extensive cabin accommodation.

Very few pioneers have been so outstandingly successful as the ULSTER MONARCH. Her war service was exceptionally varied and strenuous, ending with her use as an assault ship.

Afterwards she returned to her old route, and not until 1966 was she sold for scrap.

DATA: *Owners: Belfast Steamship Co. Ltd; Builders: Harland & Wolff, Belfast; Launched: 24 January, 1929; Entered service: 11 June, 1929; Tonnage (gross): 3,735 (later increased); Length overall: 358.8 ft; Breadth: 46.2 ft; Depth: 19 ft; Draught: 15 ft; Speed: 17 knots; Passengers: Approx. 420 first, 90 third; Engines: 2 4 stroke S.A. 10 cylinder Harland—B & W diesels 6,000 b.h.p; Screws: 2*

SOURABAYA (converted 1929): This ship was originally one of a series of five cargo liners—all named after Welsh counties—which were designed for the R.M.S.P. Far Eastern service. She then carried about 11,000 tons of cargo and 12 passengers.

Sold in 1929, she was altered out of all recognition into the whale factory ship SOURABAYA. Her accommodation was greatly enlarged and over her holds (altered to carry oil) a long factory deck was added, this being topped by a flensing deck served by a stern ramp. Thereafter her annual programme was to leave Norway each Autumn for the Antarctic, returning with her attendant catchers in the Spring. She was finally torpedoed in 1942.

DATA: *Previous name: CARMARTHENSHIRE; Owners: South Georgia Co. (Chr. Salvesen & Co.), Leith; Builders: Workman Clark & Co; Completed: 1915, converted 1929; Tonnage (gross): 10,107 (originally 7,823); Length between perps: 470.2 ft; Breadth: 58.3 ft; Depth: 35.0 ft; Speed: 13 knots; Engines: Quadruple-expansion. Four boilers, converted to oil 1918; Screws: 1*

H.M.S. LONDON (1929): This was the name ship of a class of four cruisers designed under the terms of the Washington Treaty, the others being the DEVONSHIRE, SHROPSHIRE and SUSSEX. DORSETSHIRE and NORFOLK were very similar, all these being slightly longer and less beamy than the five otherwise comparable KENT class ships. Torpedo tubes, 4 aside, were just abaft the funnels and abreast the catapult. Excellent at sea, these ships could maintain speed almost indefinitely and were unequalled by their foreign counterparts. Refitting at the outbreak of war, the LONDON served first with the Home, then the Eastern Fleet. She was scrapped in 1951.

DATA: *Builders: Portsmouth Dockyard; Launched: 14 September, 1927; Completed: 5 February, 1929; Tonnage (displacement): 9,850; Length overall: 633 ft; Breadth: 66 ft; Draught: 19 ft. (mean); Speed: 32¼ knots; Crew: 650; Engines: Parsons geared turbines, 80,000 s.h.p. 8 boilers; Screws: 4; Armament: 8–8 in., 8–4 in., 4–3 pdr. & 14 smaller guns, 8 torpedo tubes, 1 Aircraft*

BREMEN (1929): Germany's first Blue Riband holder for over 20 years, she sailed between Bremerhaven, Southampton, Cherbourg and New York, the Hamburg-built EUROPA joining her in March 1930. On her maiden voyage the BREMEN established new Westbound and Eastbound averages, the latter being 27.92 knots. The EUROPA did better eastwards, but was eclipsed by the BREMEN's 1933 effort of a Cherbourg—Ambrose Light average of 28.51 knots. She kept these records until 1936. An interesting experiment was the fitting of a catapult and mail carrying plane. In May 1941 the BREMEN was destroyed by fire after a raid on Bremerhaven.

DATA: *Owners: Norddeutscher Lloyd, Bremen; Builders: Akt. Ges. Weser, Bremen; Launched: 16 August, 1928; Maiden voyage: 16 July, 1929; Tonnage (gross): 51,656; Length overall: 938.4 ft; Breadth: 101.9 ft; Depth: 79 ft; Draught: 33.6 ft; Speed: 26.25 knots (normal); Crew: 960; Passengers: 2200 in four classes; Engines: S.R. geared turbines, 92,500 s.h.p; Screws: 4*

AMERIGO VESPUCCI (1930): Owned by the Italian Navy, this striking looking training ship has long outlived the very similar CRISTOFORO COLOMBO which was built two years earlier. Her hull, masts and rigging are of steel, and she has a sail area of 22,600 sq. ft. Her hull is exceptionally beamy, the waterline length being less than five times the beam. The tall funnel amidships also does duty as a derrick post.

Some years ago when refitted, her bows were remodelled and given less overhang, and the bowsprit restepped more steeply.

She has frequently taken part in the Sail Training Ship Race. **DATA:** *Built: at Castellammare; Launched: 22 March, 1930; Tonnage (full load displacement): 4,146; Length overall: 270 ft. (330 ft. over bowsprit); Length between perps: 229 ft. 6 ins; Breadth: 51 ft; Draught: 22 ft; Speed: 10½ knots; Crew: 400 + 150 midshipmen; Engines: Diesel-electric, 2 Fiat motors driving 2 Marelli motors, 1,900 h.p; Screws: One; Armament: 4–3 in. A.A. and 1–20 mm gun*

EMPRESS OF JAPAN (1930): The largest and most luxurious liner ever built for regular trans-Pacific service, she operated between Vancouver, Victoria, Honolulu, Yokohama and Hong Kong. After one Atlantic round voyage she went to the Pacific and there made a record breaking crossing to Canada at 21.04 knots. During wartime trooping she was renamed EMPRESS OF SCOTLAND. Post war service was in the North Atlantic. Sold Germany 1958, she became the two-funnelled HANSEATIC. After fire at New York 1966 she was towed to Hamburg and later scrapped.

DATA: *Owners: Canadian Pacific Railway Co; Builders: Fairfield Shipbuilding & Engineering Co., Govan; Launched: 17 December, 1929; Maiden voyage: 26 June, 1930; Tonnage (gross): 26,032; Length overall: 666 ft; Breadth: 83.5 ft; Depth: 65 ft. (to prom. deck); Draught: 30 ft; Speed: 21 knots (23 on trials); Crew: 580; Passengers: 400/164/100 plus 510 steerage; Engines: Parsons S.R. geared turbines, 30,000 s.h.p; 6 boilers, 425 p.s.i., 725 deg. F; Screws: 2*

AAGTEKERK (1934). Named after a small Dutch village, but designed for the Australian trade, this striking-looking cargo liner incorporated much new thinking. Besides being her owners' first motorship, she was the first to be built in Holland with the then newly developed Maierform type of hull. This improved performance and was outwardly distinguished by pronounced curve and slope to both stem and stern. Twin spade type rudders were fitted. She had six holds, and of her many derricks one could handle 80 ton loads. All deck gear was electrically driven. The AAGTEKERK, shown in the Thames, was sunk May 1942 when one of a Malta convoy.

DATA: *Owners: United Netherlands Navigation Co., The Hague; Builders: Netherlands Shipbuilding Co., Amsterdam; Completed: January 1934; Tonnage (gross): 6,811; (deadweight): 9,114; Length overall: 493 ft; Breadth: 60 ft; Depth: 40.9 ft; Draught: 28.4 ft; Speed: 16 knots; Passengers: 10; Engines: Two—6 cyl. 2 str. D.A. Stork type diesels 8,300 b.h.p., 122 r.p.m.; Screws: 2*

NORMANDIE (1935): A ship of great luxury and most advanced design, the NORMANDIE had a Yourkevitch type hull, and at 29 knots her fuel consumption was no greater than that of the 43,000 ton ILE DE FRANCE at 23½ knots. On her maiden voyage to New York she averaged a record breaking 29.98 knots, and returned at 30.35 knots. Later she did better, but eventually the QUEEN MARY proved faster. Requisitioned at New York to become the U.S. troopship LAFAYETTE, she sank there after fire February 1942, and was scrapped in 1946.

DATA: *Owners: Cie. Generale Transatlantique, Paris; Builders: Ch. & Atel. de St. Nazaire Penhoet; Launched: 29 October, 1932; Completed: 29 May, 1935; Tonnage (gross): 83,432; (displacement): 67,500; Length overall: 1029.3 ft; Breadth: 117.9 ft; Depth: 91.9 ft; Draught: 36.6 ft; Speed: 29 knots; Crew: 1345; Passengers: Approx. 850 first, 670 tourist, 450 third; Engines: Turbo-electric, 160,000 s.h.p., 29 boilers, 400 p.s.i., 600 deg. F; Screws: 4*

ORION (1935): Both in her outward appearance and interior design, the ORION broke with tradition. Instead of the unduly lavish and ornate, she was furnished throughout in a contemporary style which proved extremely popular.

Besides her novel corn-coloured hull and single mast, her open decks were exceptionally spacious and uncluttered—this through careful grouping of ventilators, winches, etc. Constant wartime use as a troopship was followed by repatriation work, but in 1947, refitted to carry 550 first and 700 tourist, she returned to her designed Australian trade.

After brief use as a Hamburg hotel ship in 1963 she was scrapped.

DATA: *Owners: Orient Steam Navigation Co; Builders: Vickers-Armstrongs, Barrow; Launched: 7 December, 1934; Completed: July 1935; Tonnage (gross): 23,371; (deadweight): 11,800; Length overall: 665 ft; Breadth: 84 ft. (extreme); Depth: 47.5 ft; Draught: 30 ft. 2 ins; Speed: 21 knots; Crew: 466; Passengers: 486 first, 653 tourist; Engines: Parsons S.R. geared turbines, 24,000 s.h.p; 6 boilers, 450 p.s.i, Screws: 2*

SHEPPERTON FERRY (1935): This ship and her sisters TWICKENHAM FERRY and HAMPTON FERRY were the first train ferries to operate from Britain in which the vehicle deck was enclosed by the superstructure. They were designed for the Dover–Dunkirk service, but this did not open until some time after their completion owing to difficulties in building the Dover Terminal. Their four rail tracks (which converge to two at the stern) can take 8 international sleeping cars or 40 25 ft. wagons. The garage (above) has space for up to 25 cars of average size. The ships, oil-fired from 1947, used to rely on coal fed by mechanical stokers. The last of them, TWICKENHAM FERRY, was scrapped in 1974. **DATA:** *Owners: Southern Railway Co; Builders: Swan, Hunter & Wigham Richardson, Newcastle; Completed: March 1935; Tonnage (gross): 2,839; Length overall: 360 ft; Breadth: 60.7 ft; Depth: 20 ft; Draught: 12 ft. 6 ins; Speed: 15 knots (service); Passengers: 800; Engines: Parsons S.R. geared turbines 5,000 s.h.p. 4 Yarrow boilers; Screws: 2*

QUEEN MARY (1936): Holder of the Blue Riband from August 1938 until the advent of the UNITED STATES in 1952. Designed for a two-ship Southampton—New York service, on which three had previously been needed. War prevented the QUEEN ELIZABETH from joining her on this until October 1946. Thereafter they operated with great success until the MARY's withdrawal in 1967. Twin stabilisers fitted 1958. Made first cruise Christmas 1963. Now a hotel-museum-convention centre at Long Beach, California.

DATA: *Owners: Cunard Steam Ship Co. Ltd; Builders: John Brown & Co. Clydebank; Launched: 26 September, 1934; Delivered: May 1936; Tonnage (gross): 80,774 (finally 81,237); Length overall: 1,019 ft. 6 ins; Length between perps: 965 ft; Breadth: 118 ft. 7 ins; Depth (to prom. deck): 92 ft. 6 ins; Draught: 38 ft. 10 ins; Speed: 28½ knots service; Crew: 1100 (later increased); Passengers: Originally 2,139, later reduced, three classes; Engines: 16 S.R. geared turbines. 24 Watertube boilers. 425 p.s.i., 700 deg. F; Screws: 4*

NIEUW AMSTERDAM (1938): A ship with a great reputation. After making 17 round trips Rotterdam–New York and some cruises, she was converted at Halifax N.S. late 1940 into a troopship able to carry 8,000. After being armed—with 36 guns—at Singapore, she saw world wide service, travelling over 530,000 miles. Undamaged, she finally returned to Rotterdam in April 1946. She resumed service October 1947. In 1961 she was again completely refitted and converted from a three- to two-class ship. Latterly a cruise liner, she was scrapped in 1974.

DATA: *Flag: Dutch; Owners: Holland-America Line, Rotterdam; Builders: Rotterdam Dry Dock Co; Launched: 10 April, 1937; Entered service: May 1938; Tonnage (gross): 36,982; Length overall: 758 ft. 6 ins; Breadth: 88 ft. 4 ins; Depth: 73 ft. (to prom. deck); Draught: 31 ft. 6 ins; Speed: 20½ knots; Crew: 770; Passengers: 1274 (cabin and tourist); Engines: S.R. geared steam turbines, 34,620 s.h.p. 5 W.T. boilers, 512 p.s.i., 750 deg. F; Screws: Two*

INVERSUIR (1938): A typical motor tanker of the period, but one of seven (all with INVER- names) whose careers were outstanding for their tragic brevity. Built in Germany—to use frozen currency—they were intended to supply a projected oil refinery at Dublin. The refinery was never built, so initially several of the INVERS had to be laid up. Then came the war and a new demand for tankers. Eight days later a U-boat sank the INVERLIFFEY, and by February 1943 all seven had been sunk. The INVERSUIR, torpedoed and shelled by an enemy submarine, went down in mid Atlantic on 2 June, 1941. Inver Tankers built no more ships.

DATA: *Owners: Inver Tankers Ltd (Andrew Weir & Co.), London; Builders: Deutsche Werft, Finkenwarder, Hamburg; Completed: November 1938; Tonnage (gross): 9,456; (deadweight): 14,000; Length overall: 522 ft; Breadth: 67.3 ft; Depth: 34.2 ft; Draught: 27 ft. 7 ins; Speed: 12 knots; Engines: One 8 cyl. 2 stroke S.A. M.A.N. diesel; Screws: One*

H.M.S. MAIDSTONE (1938): Depot ship for submarines. Sister FORTH completed a year later. Designed to provide all the accommodation, amenities and medical facilities needed for the crews of nine submarines, together with the workshops and equipment required for the maintenance of the submarines themselves. Also provided with extensive diving and salvage gear, and stocks of torpedoes and mines. Main armament (8—4.5 ins. guns) removed when reconstructed 1958-62 to support nuclear submarines. Stationed at Faslane (Clyde) until 1969 to serve Third Submarine Squadron, then laid up at Portsmouth prior to scrapping; but late 1969 was sent to Belfast to provide troop accommodation. She is the Navy's eighth MAIDSTONE.

DATA: *Builders: John Brown & Co., Clydebank; Launched: 21 October, 1937; Completed: 5 May, 1938; Tonnage (full load displacement): Originally 12,380, finally 14,000; Length overall: 530 ft. 3 ins; Breadth: 73 ft; Draught: 21 ft. 3 ins; Speed: 16 knots (max); Crew: 1160 (1500 max); Engines: Steam turbine Parsons geared turbines, 7,000 s.h.p. 4 boilers; Screws: Two; Armament: latterly 5—40 mm. A.A.*

H.M.S. BELFAST (1939): This cruiser of improved SOUTHAMPTON class was severely damaged and had her back broken by a magnetic mine in the Firth of Forth, November 1939. During reconstruction was given bulges, which brought extra protection, strength and improved steadiness. In December 1943 she helped in the sinking of the battleship SCHARNHORST, and in June 1944 she took part in the Normandy invasion. Later she was in the Pacific. During major reconstruction 1955-59 had torpedo tubes removed, and tripod masts replaced by lattice type. Was put in reserve 1963. As Britain's last cruiser of World War II, she is now retained as a floating museum in the Upper Pool, London. Sistership EDINBURGH sunk in Arctic 1942. **DATA:** *Builders: Harland & Wolff, Belfast; Completed: 3 August, 1939; Tonnage (full load displacement): 14,930; Length overall: 613 ft. 6 ins; Breadth: 69 ft. (originally 63 ft.); Draught: 23 ft; Speed: 31 knots; Crew: 710; Engines: Parsons geared turbines, 80,000 s.h.p. Four boilers; Screws: Four; Armament: 12–6 in. guns, 8–4 in. A.A., 8–40 mm. A.A.*

EMPIRE FAITH (1941): In the battle of the Atlantic it was the 500 mile middle stretch of ocean which was the most hazardous for British convoys. There, beyond the range of shore based aircraft, German U-boats and long range bombers could take their toll with minimum risk.

The C.A.M. ship (catapult equipped merchant ship) provided a temporary but costly answer. When necessary her single Hurricane fighter could take off and do battle. Afterwards, however, it had to be ditched, the pilot being picked up by

rescue ship. The EMPIRE FAITH, latterly named GLOBAL VENTURE, was broken up in 1971.

DATA: *Owners: Ministry of War Transport; Builders: Barclay Curle & Co., Glasgow; Completed: June 1941; Tonnage (gross): 7,061; (deadweight): 10,350; Length overall: 432 ft; Breadth: 57.4 ft; Depth: 38 ft; Draught: 27 ft. 6 ins; Speed: 12 knots; Passengers: None; Engines: 4 cyl. Doxford type diesel; Screws: One; Armament: Defensive only*

FRANCIS DRAKE (1942): Shown in wartime paint, this example of the famous Liberty ship has spent much of her postwar career laid up at Mobile, Alabama, as one of the U.S. Reserve Fleet.

The first Liberty ship, the PATRICK HENRY, was delivered in January 1942 and by 1945, when the series ended, about 2,700 had been built. Construction times varied according to shipyard. The average was about 40 days, but as a stunt the ROBERT E. PEARY was delivered 7 days 14 hours after keel laying. Based on a British design, they have five holds and two decks. Although originally regarded as expendable, a few were still operating in the early 1970s.

DATA: *Owners: U.S. Maritime Commission; Builders: California S.B. Corp., Los Angeles; Launched: 1942; Tonnage (gross): 7,176; (deadweight): 10.807; (displacement): 14,245; Length overall: 442 ft; Breadth: 57 ft; Depth: 37 ft; Draught: 27 ft. 9 ins; Speed: 11 knots; Crew: 54; Engines: Steam, triple expansion, 2,500 s.h.p. 2 boilers; Screws: One*

H.M.S. ANSON (1942): One of the five KING GEORGE V class battleships which also included the PRINCE OF WALES, DUKE OF YORK and HOWE. They introduced a new type 14 in. gun superior to the previous 15 in., both for rate of fire and penetrating power. The ANSON saw much wartime service in the Arctic and Norwegian waters and was one of those which provided cover for the successful air attack on the battleship TIRPITZ. Later she reinforced the Pacific Fleet. After a long lay up she went to the breakers in December 1957.

110

DATA: *Provisional name: JELLICOE; Builders: Swan Hunter & Wigham Richardson, Newcastle, Launched: 24 February, 1940; Completed: 22 June, 1942; Tonnage (full load displacement): 44,620 tons; Length overall: 745 ft; Breadth: 103 ft; Draught: 27 ft. 8 ins; Speed: 27 knots (29 max); Crew: 1,550 peace (2,000 wartime); Engines: Parsons S.R. geared turbines, 110,000 s.h.p. 8 boilers; Screws: Four; Armament: 10—14 in. guns, 16—5.25 in. dual purpose and many A.A. 4 aircraft*

U.S.S. NEW JERSEY (1943): One of the IOWA class battleships of which four were completed, the others being IOWA, MISSOURI, and WISCONSIN—work on KENTUCKY being suspended. These were the greatest of all Allied battleships, and were exceeded in size only by the Japanese YAMATO and MUSASHI of 63/64,000 tons.

The IOWA class cost approximately $100,000,000 apiece. NEW JERSEY joined the Pacific Fleet in January 1944 and during that year and 1945 she saw very strenuous action, mostly in Task Force operations. These, besides combat with enemy ships, were concerned with the seizure and holding of enemy territory.

DATA: *Builders: Philadelphia Navy yard; Launched: 7 December, 1942; Completed: 23 May, 1943; Tonnage (full load displacement): 57,600; Length overall: 887 ft. 3 ins; Breadth: 108 ft; Draught: 38 ft; Speed: 33 knots (+35 knots max), Crew: 2,700 (wartime); Engines: Geared turbines, 200,000 s.h.p. 12 boilers; Screws: Four; Armament: 9–16 in., 20–5 in. guns, 80–40 mm. A.A., 48–20 mm. A.A., 4 aircraft*

EMPIRE MACALPINE (1943): The first of the convoy protecting M.A.C. ships (Merchant Aircraft Carriers) which followed the C.A.M. ships. She and her five sisters had eight holds for grain (loaded by shute, sucked empty by elevators) and, above these, a hangar and 422 ft. long flight deck.

Four others were built to carry oil, not grain. Nine tankers were also given a flight deck and side bridge, but having no hangars they carried their planes on top. War over, all were rebuilt on commercial lines.

DATA: *Owners: Ministry of War Transport; Builders: Burntisland Shipbuilding Co; Laid down: 11 August 1942; Completed: 14 April 1943; Tonnage (gross): 7,954; (deadweight): 8,575; Length overall: 448 ft; Breadth: 57 ft; Depth: 37 ft. 9 ins; Draught: 25 ft. 8 ins; Speed: 13 knots; Crew: 52, plus 39 Fleet Air Arm and 16 defence ratings; Engines: One 4 cylinder Doxford diesel, 3,400 b.h.p; Screws: One; Defensive Armament: 1—12 pdr., 4—Oerlikons, 2 Bofors guns, 4 Swordfish aircraft*

H.M.S. LOCH FADA (1944): Of Britain's war-built frigates, the LOCHs and BAYs were probably the finest. Over 50 were built, the construction of a like number being cancelled at the end of the war. In the LOCHs the emphasis was on A.A. armament; only a single 4 in. gun being fitted. The BAYs however were intended to deal with enemy surface forces and therefore had four such guns, but less A.A. The LOCH FADA, the last of her type in the Royal Navy, was scrapped at Faslane in 1970.

DATA: *Builders: J. Brown & Co., Clydebank; Launched: 14 December, 1943; Completed: 10 April, 1944; Tonnage (full load displacement): 2,450; Length overall: 307 ft; Breadth: 38 ft. 6 ins; Draught: 14 ft. 7 ins; Speed: 19½ knots; Crew: 140; Engines: Two 4 cyl. triple expansion, 5,500 l.h.p. 2 boilers; Screws: Two; Armament: One (later two) 4 in., 6—40 mm. A.A. guns, Two triple barrelled squids*

EMPIRE CELTIC (1945): The L.S.T. (Landing Ship, Tank) resulted from the wartime need for a vessel able to carry tanks etc. and land them on open beaches. The main vehicle deck (flanked by accommodation) has a forward ramp inside the bow doors.

This L.S.T., Mark 3, was one of three chartered by Bustards in 1945—who pioneered in the commercial application of this type. Carried up to 60/100 vehicles, depending on size, and had accommodation for drivers. Operated on the Transport Ferry Services between Preston-Larne and Tilbury-Continent until new ships became ready. Scrapped 1962 in Italy.

DATA: *Previous name: L.S.T. 3512; Owners: Ministry of Transport (Managed by Frank Bustard & Sons, London); Builders: Davie S.B. & Rep. Co., Lauzon, P.Q; Launched: 25 April, 1945; Tonnage (gross): 4,291; Length overall: 345.4 ft; Breadth: 55.1 ft; Depth: 27 ft; Draught: 11 ft. 6 ins. (aft); Speed: 13 knots; Crew: 50; Engines: Two 4 cyl. Triple expansion, 5,500 l.h.p, 2 Watertube boilers. Screws: Two*

H.M.S. VANGUARD (1946): Britain's final and greatest battleship, and bearer of a name with battle honours dating back to the Armada. Ordered under the War Estimates, her design was not hampered by treaty restrictions. Cost £9,000,000 exclusive of guns and mountings. Her 15 in. guns were originally fitted in the COURAGEOUS and GLORIOUS of World War I. Had armour up to 14 ins. thick and four separate engine rooms.

In 1947 was used for Royal tour to South Africa. After Mediterranean service became Flagship of the Home Fleet 1952-54. Was at Portsmouth from 1956 in operational Reserve, and in 1960 was scrapped at Faslane.

DATA: *Builders: John Brown & Co., Clydebank; Launched: 30 November, 1944; Completed: 25 April, 1946; Tonnage (full load displacement): 51,420; Length overall: 814 ft. 4 ins; Breadth: 108 ft. 6 ins; Draught: 36 ft; Speed: 29.5 knots; Crew: 1,600 (peacetime); Engines: Parsons S.R. geared turbines, 130,000 s.h.p. 8 boilers; Screws: Four; Armament: 8- 15 in., 16—5.25 in., 60—40 mm. A.A.*

CARONIA (1949): Britain's largest post-war liner, and named by the Queen when Princess Elizabeth. Owners' title then Cunard White Star Ltd. Their first with a green hull, she was designed primarily for long cruises with seasonal use on the Atlantic. Original tonnage and passenger figures given. First class later reduced and tourist (formerly cabin) correspondingly increased, but ship always one class when cruising. Major improvements made 1965-6.

She was sold abroad in 1968 and renamed first COLUMBIA, then CARIBIA, but cruise plans were killed by an early acci-

dent. Long idle at New York, she left in April 1974 bound—in tow—for Eastern breakers, but was wrecked en route.

DATA: *Owners: Cunard Line; Builders: John Brown & Co., Clydebank; Launched: 30 October, 1947; Entered service: January 1949; Tonnage (gross): 34,183; Length overall: 715 ft; Breadth: 91 ft. 5 ins; Depth: 70 ft. 3 ins. (to prom. deck); Draught: 31 ft. 7 ins; Speed: 22 knots; Crew: 587; Passengers: 581 first, 381 cabin class; Engines: (High pressure D.R. geared, others S.R. geared), 35,000 s.h.p; 6 boilers; Screws: Two*

ANGELIKA (acquired 1949): Named after her owner's mother, this ship became well known on the Brindisi—Corfu—Piraeus route. Her purchase in 1949 with two others from Canadian Pacific was a major event in the rebirth of the Greek passenger fleet, after its wartime destruction. It also marked Typaldos Lines' entry into the tourist trade. Her style of decor, though novel to Europe, was typical of the North Pacific. Built to carry 1,200 passengers, she had previously operated on the Vancouver—Victoria night run, on the "triangle" route (which included Seattle) and also Northwards to Alaska.

The ANGELIKA was sold to Italian breakers in 1967.

DATA: *Previous name: PRINCESS ADELAIDE; Owners: Aegaean Steam Navigation Typaldos Bros. Ltd., Piraeus; Builders: Fairfield, Glasgow; Launched: 10 July 1910; Tonnage (gross): 3,061; Length overall: 299 ft. 9 ins; Breadth: 46 ft; Draught: 13 ft; Speed: Originally 18 knots; Passengers: 340 berthed, plus deck; Engines: 4 cylinder steam Triple expansion, oil fired boilers; Screws: One*

HACKNEY (1952): It has been on colliers such as this that London's power stations and gas works have long depended for their supplies from the North East Coast. Owing to the growing use of oil (and nuclear power) the collier as a type is fast dwindling in numbers, and the HACKNEY herself was sold in the early 1970s. Designed to serve up-river power stations and negotiate low bridges, she was of the "flat-iron" type, with hinged funnel, telescopic mast and minimum of superstructure. Her three holds were of self-trimming design and specially shaped for quick loading and grab discharge.

DATA: *Owners: Central Electricity Generating Board, London (Managers: Stephenson Clarke Ltd.); Builders: S.P. Austin & Son Ltd., Sunderland; Completed: March 1952; Tonnage (gross): 1,782; (deadweight): 2,690; Length overall: 270 ft. 6 ins; Breadth: 39 ft. 6 ins; Depth: 18 ft. 6 ins; Draught: 17 ft. 1 in; Speed: 10½ knots; Crew: 19; Engines: Reciprocating. Triple expansion, 950 l.h.p. 1 coal-fired boiler, 200 lbs. pressure; Screws: One*

UNITED STATES (1952): America's largest liner and by far the world's fastest. On her maiden voyage she made record-breaking crossings in each direction, the Eastward average being 35.59 knots. She operated between New York—Le Havre—Southampton, often continuing to Bremerhaven; but also made some cruises. Service requirements featured largely in her design, this for quick and efficient conversion into troopship—hence her all-metal equipment (the piano and butcher's block being reputedly the only exceptions). She was withdrawn from commercial service in November 1969 and subsequently laid up.

DATA: *Owners: United States Lines Co., New York; Builders: Newport News S.B. & D.D. Co; Launched: 23 June 1951 (floated out of graving dock); Maiden voyage: July 1952; Tonnage (gross): Originally 53,329 (later reduced); Length overall: 990 ft; Breadth: 101 ft. 6 ins; Depth: 122 ft. (to top of superstructure); Draught: 31 ft; Speed: 30-32 knots (in service) 42 max; Crew: 1,000; Passengers: 1,926; Engines: 4, Steam turbines, D.R. geared. 240,000 h.p; Screws: Four, five bladed*

OLYMPIA (1953): The largest passenger ship to be built for Greece, she introduced a new streamlined appearance, besides setting new standards for tourist class travel. She made her maiden sailing from Southampton to New York in October 1953. With Bremerhaven as her terminal, she remained on the Atlantic until 1955. In later years she operated on the Mediterranean—New York route with the QUEEN ANNA MARIA, the two subsequently being used for cruises. Their active careers may well be over, for since March 1974 and January 1974 respectively they have been laid up at Piraeus. Essentially a tourist class ship, her passengers had 5 decks, and seventeen public rooms the first class being mainly on the sun and promenade decks.

DATA: *Flag: Greek; Owners: Transatlantic Shipping Corporation (Greek Line, Piraeus); Builders: Alex. Stephen & Sons, Glasgow; Launched: April 1953; Tonnage (gross): 17,269; Length overall: 610 ft. 7 ins; Breadth: 79 ft. 2 ins; Depth: 47 ft; Draught: 28 ft. 1 in; Speed: 21 knots; Passengers: 1350; Engines: Steam turbines, D.R. geared, 25,000 s.h.p; Screws: Two*

H.M.S. DIANA (1954): The last of the eight DARING class destroyers to be completed for the Royal Navy. In this class was introduced a new type of radar controlled gun; these were mounted in twin turrets and proved capable of very rapid and accurate fire—both against ships and aircraft. DIANA's original ten 21 inch torpedo tubes were later removed.

The DARINGs were the largest and last destroyers to be built for R.N.; although excellent, their high cost and large crews at present show frigates to advantage. Late 1969 the DIANA—the last British one in commission—was sold to Peru. Three of this class were built in Australia, and their VOYAGER when sunk was replaced by the British DUCHESS.

DATA: *Builders: Yarrow & Co., Scotstown; Launched: May 1952; Completed: March 1954; Tonnage (full load displacement): 3,610; Length overall: 390 ft; Breadth: 43 ft; Draught: 18 ft; Speed: 30.5 knots (sea); Crew: Approx. 300; Engines: Steam turbines, 54,000 s.h.p; Boilers: 2, 650 p.s.i., 850 deg. F; Screws: 2; Armament: Six 4.5 in. guns, two 40 mm. A.A., one 3-barrelled A/S mortar*

LEOPOLDO PERES (1954): This shallow draft passenger and cargo ship was one of four sisters built in Holland for use in the various rivers of the Amazon system. Belem is their down-river limit. The others are named AUGUSTO MONTENEGRO, LAURO SODRE and LOBO D'ALMADI, all after Brazilians, in recognition of their work in developing the Amazon region. The accommodation is spread over four decks, and there is also space for 500 tons of cargo.

With her main deck boarded up, the PERES made the delivery voyage from Rotterdam to Belem in 18 days.

DATA: *Flag: Brazilian; Owners: Servicos de Navegacao de Amazonia e de Administracao do Porto do Para; Builders: N.V. Scheepswerf Gebr. van der Werf, Deest, Holland; Launched: April 18, 1954; Tonnage (gross): 1,352; Length overall: 233 ft. 7 ins; Breadth: 42 ft. 1 in; Depth: 10 ft. 6 ins. (to main deck); Draught: 7 ft. 10 ins; Speed: 12 knots; Crew: 30; Passengers: 96 first class, 300 third (deck) class; Engines: 2 6 cyl Sulzer diesels, 1,300 b.h.p. at 325 r.p.m; Screws: Two*

H.M.S. ALBION (1954): Converted at Portsmouth 1961-62 from aircraft carrier to Commando ship, after experience gained with conversion of sister BULWARK.

Designed to carry a full strength Commando and its equipment and land it wherever required. Commando messes, all gear and stores were located close to lift for quickest loading into helicopters, which could also lift vehicles to and from shore. These helicopters could also be modified on board for anti-submarine duties. ALBION also carried four L.C.A.s. Her service career ended November 1972 and a year later she was scrapped at Faslane.

DATA: *Builders: Swan Hunter & Wigham Richardson, Wallsend-on-Tyne; Launched: 6 May, 1947; Completed: 26 May, 1954; Tonnage (full load displacement): 27,300; Length overall: 737 ft. 9 ins; Breadth: 123 ft. 6 ins; Draught: 28 ft; Speed: 28 knots; Crew: Approx. 1,030 + 730 Royal Marines; Engines: Parsons geared turbines, 78,000 s.h.p. 4 boilers; Screws: Two; Armament: 8—40 mm. A.A., 4—3 pdr. guns. About 16 helicopters*

SOUTHERN CROSS (1955): This ship, launched by the Queen, was the first British passenger liner to have engines aft. She maintained a round-the-world service between Southampton, Australia and New Zealand, normally sailing westabout, while the NORTHERN STAR (built 1962) went eastabout. To reduce port delays they carried no cargo and the resultant time saved enabled them to make four round voyages per year, one more than cargo ships of similar speed. Both vessels carried tourist class only and had exceptionally spacious decks. The SOUTHERN CROSS, sold 1974, became the Greek cruise liner CALYPSO. A year later the NORTHERN STAR was withdrawn.

DATA: *Owners: Shaw Savill & Albion Co., London; Builders: Harland & Wolff, Belfast; Launched: 17 August, 1954; Completed: February 1955; Tonnage (gross): 20,204, (later 19,313); Length overall: 603 ft. 10 ins; Breadth: 80 ft. 1 in; Depth: 45 ft. 3 ins; Draught: 25 ft. 10 ins; Speed: 20 knots; Crew: 410 (approx); Passengers: 1,185; Engines: D.R. geared turbines, 20,000 s.h.p. 3 WT boilers; Screws: Two*

GIRDLE NESS (converted 1956): A ship which had a brief period of fame. Shown as a Guided Missiles Trials Ship, the role she held from 1956 to 1961. Was laid down as a standard FORT/PARK type freighter, but altered while building to become a Landing Craft Maintenance Ship.

Conversion into a trials ship for the "Seaslug" missile was carried out at Devonport, and lasted from October 1953 to July 1956. The triple missile launcher was fitted forward; the superstructure and masts were altered and new radar

installed. When paid off she went to Rosyth to form part of the COCHRANE establishment.

DATA: *Builders: Burrand Dry Dock Co. Ltd., North Vancouver; Launched: 29 March, 1945; Completed: September, 1945; Tonnage (full load displacement): 10,200 tons; Length overall: 441 ft; Breadth: 57 ft; Draught: 20 ft; Speed: 10 knots; Crew: 400 (up to 616 for trials); Engines: Steam, Triple expansion, 2,500 l.h.p.; Screws: 1; Armament: 1 triple "Seaslug" launcher*

JOSEPH S. YOUNG (converted 1957): This ship operated as a T2 tanker until 1956-7, when she was converted, as shown, into a Great Lakes bulk carrier of 14,000 tons deadweight. The old bow and bridge were removed, and a new forward half-ship joined on. To reach the Lakes (through low bridges) the after superstructure was stowed in layers on deck. From her present hopper-shaped holds, cargo falls onto a conveyor, to flow at up to 4,000 tons per hour along a 250 ft. discharge boom.

Lengthened by another 100 ft. in 1966, she now has 34 hatches: Her present name (since 1969) is H. LEE WHITE.

DATA: *Previous name:* ARCHERS HOPE; *Owners: American S.S. Co. Inc. Buffalo;* *Builders:* Alabama S.B. & D.D. Co., Mobile; *Completed:* 1945, *Tonnage (gross): 10,497/12,489/14,452;* *Length overall: 523 ft./572 ft./672 ft. 10 ins;* *Breadth:* 68 ft. 2 ins; *Depth: 39 ft. 3 ins;* *Draught: 30 ft./27 ft. 7 ins./26 ft. 9 ins; Engines: Turbo-electric, 6,000 s.h.p; Screws: One.*

*Note: these show progressive enlargement (length and tonnage) but draught reduction

H.M.S. BRAVE BORDERER (1958): The first of a notable class of gas turbine driven Fast Patrol Boats (F.P.B.s), she was followed by BRAVE SWORDSMAN, BRAVE PATHFINDER and BRAVE PIONEER. In size midway between the 71 ft. DARK class and the 122 ft. BOLDs, they were designed for offensive action against enemy shipping in coastal and shallow waters. Their gas turbines were a marine version of those used in the BRITANNIA aircraft and developed exceptionally high power in relation to weight. Gun turrets were power operated. Armament could be varied as required.

DATA: *Builders: Vosper Ltd., Portsmouth; Launched: 7 January, 1958; Joined R. Navy: 20 July, 1960; Tonnage (full load displacement): 114; Length overall: 98 ft. 10 ins; Breadth: 25 ft. 6 ins; Draught: 6 ft. 3 ins. (mean); Speed: over 50 knots (trials); Crew: 20 Engines: 3 Bristol Marine Proteus gas turbine units, 10,500 s.h.p., Screws: 3; Armament: As MTB 4–2 in. torpedoes, 1–40 mm. Bofors gun or as MGB 2 torpedoes and 2 single 40 mm. Bofors guns*

ROTTERDAM (1959): When commissioned her severe external shaping with twin uptakes provided a refreshing contrast to previous conservative styles. Holland's largest passenger ship, she is now one of the world's most popular and luxurious cruise ships. Her current voyages vary from weekly cruises from the U.S.A. to Bermuda and the Bahamas to medium and long distance ones. She is specially famed for her world voyages and that scheduled for 1976 will be her 18th. The slim dark vertical lines along the superstructure are the coverings for the expansion joints. The

light grey topsides shown are now painted a dark blue.

DATA: *Owners: Holland-America Line, Rotterdam; Builders: Rotterdam Dry Dock Co; Launched: 13 September, 1958; Completed: August 1959; Tonnage (gross): 38,621; Length overall: 748 ft. 7 ins; Length between perps: 650 ft; Breadth: 94 ft. 2 ins; Depth: 54 ft. 9 ins. (to main deck); Draught: 29 ft. 8 ins; Speed: 21½ knots; Crew: 775; Passengers: from 800 to 1,050, depending on duration; Engines: D.R. geared turbines, 38,500 s.h.p. 4 boilers, 710 p.s.i., 865 deg. F; Screws: Two*

ORIANA (1960): A ship of revolutionary design, she was launched by Princess Alexandra of Kent. She was Britain's first liner with a bulbous bow, also the last to be launched for the Orient Line—amalgamation with P. & O. taking place before her completion. Is five knots faster than previous ships, and cut passage time U.K.—Australia by one week. Mechanically she is outstandingly efficient and on trials did 30.64 knots. Now a very popular cruise ship.

Aluminium superstructure. Her forward electric cranes travel on thwartship rails. Five holds.

DATA: *Owners: P & O Steam Navigation Co; Builders: Vickers-Armstrongs, Barrow-in-Furness; Launched: 3 November, 1959; Entered service: December 1960; Tonnage (gross): 41,915; Length overall: 804 ft; Length between perps: 740 ft; Breadth: 97 ft. 2 ins; Depth: 41 ft. 10 ins; Draught: 32 ft; Speed: 27½ knots; Crew: 889; Passengers: 1,700 open (first) class; Engines: D.R. geared turbines, 80,000 s.h.p. (Max); 4 boilers, 905 p.s.i., 960 deg. F; Screws: Two, plus thwartship propulsion units forward and aft*

WINDSOR CASTLE (1960): Launched by the Queen Mother. Her builders' biggest liner and the largest one ever built for the South African trade. On this Union-Castle and Safmarine mail ships leave Southampton on Thursdays at 13.00 hours, the passage to the Cape taking 11½ days. All tourist recreation spaces and public rooms (dining rooms excepted) are on one deck, the first class likewise, but one deck higher. Cargo capacity large, with much of it insulated. Now the largest of the few liners which still operate full-time on their designed trade.

DATA: *Owners: Union-Castle Line; Builders; Cammell Laird, Birkenhead; Launched: 23 June, 1959; Entered service: 18 August, 1960; Tonnage (gross): 36,123; Length overall: 783 ft. 1 in; Breadth: 92 ft. 6 ins; Depth: 50 ft. (to C. deck); Draught: 32 ft. 1 in; Speed: 23½ knots; Crew: approx. 475; Passengers: 242 first, 585 tourist (some interchangeable); Engines: S.R. geared turbines, 49,400 s.h.p. (max), 3 boilers, 700 p.s.i., 950 deg. F; Screws: Two*

CANBERRA (1961): Cost over £15 million. Keel laid September 1957, five days after ORIANA. Although intended for the same service, their appearance could hardly have been more different. Special features include top decks clear of lifeboats, terraced afterside of bridge overlooking midship lido area; also placing of public room decks above and below two decks of cabins. Three swimming pools for passengers, also one for crew forward. Now used solely for cruising.

Owners: P & O Steam Navigation Co; Builders: Harland & Wolff, Belfast; Launched: 16 March 1960; Entered service: June 1961; Tonnage (gross): 45,733; Length overall: 818 ft. 6 ins; Length between perps: 740 ft; Breadth: 102 ft. 6 ins; Depth: 41 ft. 6 ins; Draught: 32 ft. 6 ins; Speed: 26½ knots; Crew: 938; Passengers: 1,760 open (first) class; Engines: Turbo-electric, 85,000 s.h.p. 3 main boilers, 750 p.s.i., 960 deg. F. 1 aux. boiler (750/900); Screws: Two, plus bow propulsion unit

131

FRANCE (1962): Still the world's largest liner. Cost £30 million, her owners paying £23 million, the rest being Government subsidy. Ordered 25 July 1956. Maiden voyage to New York 3 February, 1962. Tourist class so good that little different from First. Eleven decks, nine for passengers. Method I fire protection used, all materials being incombustible. In cross-winds funnels discharge smoke leeward side. Two sets of stabilisers. Trial speed over 34 knots. Withdrawn 1974 and laid up at Le Havre.

DATA: *Owners: Cie. Generale Transatlantique, Paris,*

Builders: Chantier de l'Atlantique, Penhoit Yard, St. Nazaire; Launched: 11 May, 1960; Inaugural Cruise: 20 January, 1962; Tonnage (gross): 66,348 (full load displacement): 57,500; Length overall: 1,035 ft. 2 ins; Length between perps: 951 ft. 6 ins; Breadth: 110 ft. 11 ins; Depth: 92 ft. 2 ins. (to verandah deck); Draught: 34 ft. 5 ins; Speed: 31 knots (service); Crew: Approx. 1,000; Passengers· 500 first, 1,500 tourist (N. Atlantic); 1,200 cruising; Engines: S.R. geared turbines (115,000 s.h.p. normal, 160,000 max). 8 boilers, 914 p.s.i., 932 deg. F; Screws: Four

ORCADIA (1962): This vessel was built for regular service between the more northerly of the Orkney Islands group—where weather conditions can be exceptionally stormy. She is fitted to carry vehicles, cattle, general cargo and passengers. While engaged in normal trading she can carry up to 160 deck passengers, this number being increased to 250 for summer inter-island excursions. For first class passengers there is an observation lounge, saloon and cafeteria, also six 2-berth cabins. The vehicle deck is arranged to take 100 cattle or 600 lambs—access being by means of side doors. For cargo handling there is one 5-ton derrick.

DATA: *Owners: The Secretary of State for Scotland (Mgrs: Orkney Islands Shpg. Co.); Builders: Hall Russell & Co., Aberdeen, Completed: June 1962; Tonnage (gross): 895; Length overall: 164 ft; Breadth: 36 ft; Depth: 13.5 ft. (to vehicle deck); Speed: 12 knots; Passengers: 160 (normal trading); Engines: One 6 cyl. 2 stroke direct reversing British Polar diesel, 1,230 b.h.p; Screws: One*

SAVANNAH (1962): The world's first nuclear powered merchant ship, she was intended to demonstrate the peaceful application of nuclear power, also the feasibility of its use afloat. Economic superiority was neither hoped for nor achieved. After making a series of demonstration voyages, she was used on the U.S.A.–Mediterranean trade.

Her reactor is charged with 682,000 thimble-sized pellets of enriched uranium. These weigh 17,000 lbs. and provide energy for 16,000 hours of full power, steaming—for which 90,000 tons of oil would otherwise be needed. Her cruising

radius is 336,000 miles. The reactor is positioned low, ahead of the bridge. Since late 1970 this ship has been laid up.

DATA: *Owners: First Atomic Ship Transport Inc; Builders: New York S.B. Co., Camden; Launched: 21 July 1959; Maiden voyage: August 1952 Cargo capacity: 9,400 tons; Tonnage (gross): 15,585; Length overall: 595 ft. 6 ins; Breadth: 78 ft; Depth: 41 ft; Draught: 29 ft. 7 ins; Speed: 20¼ knots; Crew: 110, Passengers: 60; Engines: Nuclear reactor and steam turbines, 22,000 s.h.p; Screws: One*

ELIZABETHPORT (converted 1962): This ship incorporates the stern (with machinery) and bow of a former tanker and is one of the large fleet converted by Sea-Land for their various American coastwise container services. Her name is that of the specially laid out container port near New York, from which their services radiate. Her mid-body, one of several ordered in Germany, was towed to the States before re-assembly. In her new guise the ship carries up to 474 containers, both in cellular holds and on deck. They are handled by two 20-ton travelling gantries.

DATA: *Previous names: NEW ORLEANS, ESSO NEW ORLEANS; Owners: Sea-Land Service Inc., Elizabeth, N.J; Builders: (Original hull) Sun, Chester, Pa. (midbody), Schlieker, Hamburg; Completed: end portions 1942, midbody 1962; Tonnage (gross): 16,395; (deadweight): 15,770; Length overall: 627 ft. (prev. 520); Breadth: 78 ft. (prov. 68); Depth: 47 ft. (prov. 39); Draught: 27 ft; Speed: 16 knots; Engines: S.R. geared turbines, 10,000 s.h.p; Screws: One*

SHOTA RUSTAVELI (1963): The Russian ocean-going trawler fleet is the largest in the world. It includes both conventional side-fishing vessels and larger stern-ramp factory type trawlers—a type first introduced in the late 'fifties. For their construction Russia relies mainly on other nations, notably Poland and East Germany. The SHOTA RUSTAVELI is one of the TROPIK class, of which over 90 were built on a flow line production system, at Stralsund, East Germany over the period 1960-68. She and her sisters are designed to fish for sardines, herring and tunny in both

the Atlantic and the Pacific. They have extensive deep freeze storage space, with two holds forward and one aft of the main machinery.

DATA: *Owners: U.S.S.R.; Builders: Volkeswerft Stralsund, Stralsund. Completed: 1963; Tonnage (gross): 2,435; (deadweight): 1,275; Length overall: 261 ft; Breadth: 43.3 ft; Depth: 23 ft; Draught: 16 ft; Speed: 11.75 knots; Crew: About 80; Engines: 2–8 cyl. Liebknecht diesels, 1,660 b.h.p., geared to one shaft; Screws: 1*

H.M.S. HAMPSHIRE (1963): Although officially described as guided missile destroyers, the handsome "County" class ships are virtually cruisers. The others of this design are named ANTRIM, DEVONSHIRE, FIFE, GLAMORGAN, KENT, LONDON and NORFOLK. Of excellent design, they combine good hitting power with great endurance. Their machinery installation is exceptionally light and compact, and through the use of two G.6 gas turbines (each developing 7,500 s.h.p.) steam can be raised in only a few minutes. HAMPSHIRE's impending pay-off was announced 1975.

DATA: *Builders: John Brown & Co., Clydebank; Launched: 16 March, 1961, Completed: 15 March, 1963; Tonnage (full load displacement): 6,200, Length overall: 520.5 ft; Breadth: 54 ft; Draught: 20 ft; Speed: 32 knots; Crew: 470; Engines: 2 sets steam geared turbines; these boosted by 4 gas turbines, 60,000 s.h.p. total. 2 boilers; Screws: 2; Armament: 4—4.5 in. guns. 1 twin launcher (aft) for "Sleaslug" long-range guided missiles. 2 quad. launchers for short-range "Seacat" missiles, 1 Wessex helicopter*

RONDEGGEN (1963): Her cargo gear excepted, this ship—a single decker—resembles a handy sized bulk carrier. In fact she is a specialist vessel designed for the carriage of rolls of newsprint. Incorporated in the Munck gantries—which travel along fore and aft tracks—are cranes which move in a lateral direction. Each of the gantries has hinged jibs which give the necessary outreach for the cranes to load/discharge from shore. To protect the cargo from rain damage during these operations each gantry has plastic roofing and side curtains.

The cranes can lift 13½ tons apiece and a discharge rate of 1,000 tons per hour has been claimed.

DATA: *Owners: Rederiet Storeggen A/S., (Chr. Ostberg) Oslo; Builders: Kaldnaes Mek. Verk A/S., Tonsberg; Launched: 3 May, 1963; Tonnage (gross): 7,408; (deadweight): 9,180 Length overall: 459 ft; Breadth: 64 ft; Depth: 34 ft; Draught: 25 ft. 5 ins; Speed: 15 knots; Engines: One Stork 6 cyl. 2 str. S.A. diesel, 5,880 b.h.p; Screws: 1*

RAFFAELLO (1964); Together, she and her sistership MICHELANGELO (shown above) were the largest and fastest on the New York—Mediterranean route. The passage time from Genoa was 7 days. They were the first Italian liners for many years to have two funnels. All first class accommodation was in the superstructure amidships, with cabin class aft of amidships and tourist forward and aft. All cabins had private facilities. Had 30 public rooms, six outdoor swimming pools, with infra-red heating for first class lido. Two sets of stabilisers. Both ships were laid up in 1975.

DATA: *Owners: Italia Line, Genoa; Builders: Cantieri Riuniti dell'Adriatico, Trieste; Launched: 24 March, 1963; Maiden voyage: 25 July, 1964; Tonnage (gross): 45,933; Length overall: 904 ft. 7 ins; Length between perps: 800 ft. 6 ins; Breadth: 101 ft. 10 ins; Depth: 51 ft. 9 ins; Draught: 30 ft. 7 ins; Speed: 26½ knots (service); Crew: 725; Passengers: 535 first, 550 cabin, 690 tourist; Engines: 4 steam turbines, 87,000 s.h.p. 4 boilers 900 lbs. p.s.i., 914 deg. F; Screws: Two*

H.M.S. FEARLESS (1965): One of two very versatile Assault ships, the other being the INTREPID (completed March 1967).

Aft there is a large floodable dock in which four landing craft (L.C.M.s) are carried, four smaller ones being handled by davits. With the helicopters, these are able to land tanks, wheeled vehicles and troops. 400 troops can be accommodated on board the FEARLESS, and about 700 for short spells.

140

DATA: *Builders: Harland & Wolff, Belfast; Completed: 25 November, 1965; Tonnage (full load displacement): 12,120; Length overall: 520 ft; Breadth: 80 ft; Draught: 20 ft. 6 ins; (32 ft. aft when dock flooded); Speed: 21 knots; Crew: 580, plus 700 Royal Marines and Army (short periods); Engines: 2 sets English Electric turbines, 22,000 s.h.p., 2 boilers; Screws: 2; Armament: 4—Seacat A.A. missile launchers, 2—40 mm. A.A. guns; Aircraft: 5 Wessex helicopters*

JULES VERNE (1965): This methane carrier, the first of her type to be built in France, is designed to operate between Arzew (near Oran) and Le Havre, carrying LNG (liquified natural gas) from the Hassi B' Mel gas well. She has 7 cylindrical gas tanks, with a capacity of 900,000 cu. ft. and in them carries her cargo at a temperature of -160 deg. C (-265 deg. F) at approximately atmosphere pressure. Now numerous, liquified gas tankers vary considerably in appearance. In some the cylinders are entirely below deck; in others they are arranged vertically, with tops protruding (as here) or horizontally with the top ones on deck.

DATA: *Owners: Gaz Maritime, Paris; Builders: A. & C. de la Seine Maritime, Le Trait; Launched: 8 September, 1964; Completed: January 1965; Tonnage (gross): 22,292; (deadweight): 13,877; Length overall: 659.5 ft; Breadth: 81.6 ft; Depth: 54.6 ft; Draught: 24.7 ft; Speed: 17 knots; Engines: Parsons S.R. geared turbines, 12,000 s.h.p; Screws: One, plus side-thruster forward*

141

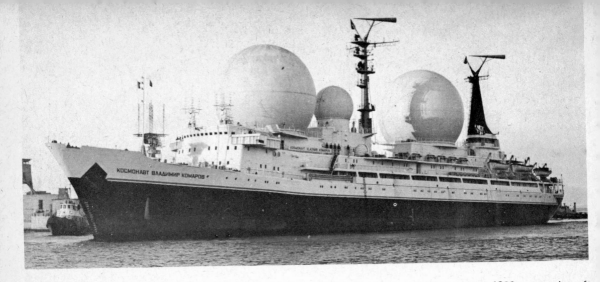

KOSMONAUT VLADIMIR KOMAROV (1966): The largest of Russia's many research ships and the only one of her type, the KOMAROV is said to be equipped for the study of the higher layers of the atmosphere in the tropical zone of the Western Atlantic. Her frequent presence in the Caribbean could well also have been linked with the monitoring of U.S. space flights from Cape Kennedy. Official information concerning Russian Naval and research ships is negligible, but it is known that the KOMAROV has a modified POLTAVA class hull with sponsons added to increase beam. The

POLTAVAs, built at Kherson since 1962, are engines-aft cargo ships which, apart from one heavy derrick rely on cranes for cargo handling.

DATA: *Previous name: GENICHESK, 1967; Owners: Soviet Academy of Sciences; Builders: Kherson Shipyard (Black Sea); Completed: 1966; Tonnage (gross): 13,935; Length overall: 510 ft. 9 ins; Breadth: 68 ft. (excluding sponsons); Speed: 17 knots; Engines: 2 Bryansk—B. & W. 7 cyl. diesels 9,000 b.h.p; Screws: One (?)*

TAUPO (1966): This highly specialised cargo liner, first owned by the N.Z.S., now forms part of the P & O fleet, as do her sisters TEKOA, TONGARIRO and WESTMORLAND. Over 480,000 cu. ft. (nearly all) of their cargo space is insulated, and especial care has been given to the cargo handling aspect—this so that their high sea speed is matched by minimum time in port. The TAUPO and her sisters were the first British ships to have a full set of Hallen masts. These, which are of the D-loop type, give very much greater control of derrick movement.

DATA: *Owners: New Zealand Shipping Co., London; Builders: Bartram & Sons, Sunderland, Launched: 27 August, 1965; Ran trials: 15 March, 1966; Tonnage (gross): 10,983; (deadweight): 11,325; Length overall: 527 ft. 7 ins; Breadth: 71 ft. 3 ins; Depth: 44 ft. 6 ins; Draught: 29 ft. 8 ins; Service speed: 20 knots; Crew: 47; Engines: 1 8 cyl. Sulzer type diesel, 2 stroke S.A., 17,600 b.h.p; Screws: 1*

H.M.S. VALIANT (1966): This was Britain's first nuclear submarine to have machinery of British design and construction, that of the prototype DREADNOUGHT (completed 1963) being American. Later units of the VALIANT class are named WARSPITE, CHURCHILL, CONQUEROR and COURAGEOUS. Equipped like DREADNOUGHT with sonar gear of extra long range, they are designed for Fleet use, mainly to hunt and destroy enemy submarines. In April 1967 the VALIANT made a record 28 day non-stop submerged voyage home from Singapore—a distance of 12,000 miles. The hump-backed profile is a distinguishing feature of all British nuclear submarines.

DATA: *Builders: Vickers Ltd. Shipbuilding Group, Barrow; Launched: 3 December, 1963; Completed: 18 July, 1966; Tonnage (displacement): 3,500/4,500; Length: 285 ft; Breadth: 33.2 ft; Draught: 27 ft; Speed: Approx. 30 knots; Crew: About 13 officers, 90 ratings; Engines: 1 pressurised water-cooled nuclear reactor with English Electric steam geared turbines; Screws: 1; Armament: 6—21 in. torpedo tubes (homing torpedoes)*

LEOPARD (1968): Fly and you have a seat only, travel by this new breed of ship—the passenger ferry—and you have the amenities of a liner plus the ability to take your car with you. The LEOPARD and her near-sister DRAGON (owned by Southern Ferries) operate between Southampton and Le Havre. Able to carry all types of road vehicles, they have exceptionally good passenger accommodation. Their companions, EAGLE and S.F. PANTHER, which covered other routes from Southampton were withdrawn late 1975.

DATA: *Operators: Normandy Ferries; Owners: Soc. Anon. de Gerance et d'Armement (S.A.G.A.); Builders: A. & C. de Bretagne & Dubigeon-Normandie S.A., Nantes; Launched: 3 November, 1967; Completed: May 1968; Tonnage (gross): 6,014; Length overall: 441 ft. 8 ins; Breadth: 71 ft. 9 ins; Depth: 38 ft. 6 ins; Draught: 15 ft. 10 ins; Speed: 19 knots; Passengers: Sleeping accom. for 500, 850 max; Vehicles: 250 cars or 65 freight units; Engines: 2 vec 12 cyl. Pielstick type diesels, 4 str. S.A., 8,900 h.p Screws: 2*

TRALEE BAY (1968): This powerful tug is one of four built for service in Bantry Bay for the handling of the giant tankers which use the Whiddy Island terminal. She is shown while escorting the UNIVERSE IRELAND—then the world's largest—on her first visit. THE DINGLE BAY was also built by Dunston's, while the BANTRY BAY and the BRANDON BAY came from the adjacent Holmes yard. Each tug has a bollard pull of 30 tons. To achieve maximum thrust the propeller is set in a Kort nozzle. Equipped for firefighting

and salvage work, they also have detergent spraying gear to deal with any oil spills.

DATA: *Flag: Irish Republic; Owners: Bantry Bay Towing Co. Ltd. (part of the Ocean Group); Builders: R. Dunston (Hessle) Ltd; Completed: July 1968; Gross Tonnage: 299, Length overall: 129 ft. 1 in; Breadth: 29 ft. 11 ins; Draught: 12 ft. 3 ins; Speed: 12½ knots; Crew: about 10; Engines: One 6 cyl. National Mirrlees diesel 2,520 b.h.p; gearing reduces 525 r.p.m. to 160 r.p.m; Screws: One*

UNIVERSE IRELAND (1968): The first of six tankers—the world's largest when new—built for National Bulk Carriers (part of the Ludwig Group) for long term charter to Gulf Oil. They carry crude oil from Kuwait to a million-ton deepwater terminal in Bantry Bay, the round voyage taking two months. Smaller tankers then distribute it to *Gulf* Refineries in Denmark, Holland, and at Milford Haven.

She has 22 tanks (capacity 312,000 tons/78 million gallons), a bulbous bow, twin rudders, five bladed propellers and hull plating up to 35 m.m. thick.

DATA: *Flag: Liberian; Owners: Bantry Transportation Co. (National Bulk Carriers); Builders: Ishikawajima—Harima Heavy Industries; Launched: 29 March, 1968; Completed: 24 August, 1968; Tonnage (gross): 149,609; Length overall: 1,132 ft. 10 ins; Breadth: 175 ft. 2 ins; Depth: 105 ft; Draught: 81 ft. 5 ins; Speed: 16 knots; Crew: 52; Engines: S.R. geared turbines, 36,000 s.h.p. (max); 2 boilers, 900 p.s.i., 960 deg. F; Screws: Two*

ATLANTIC CAUSEWAY (1969): A C L is a consortium of five (formerly six) major companies, the Cie. Generale Transatlantique, Cunard and Swedish-America Lines, also two other Swedish concerns, the Transatlantic and Wallenius Lines. In contrast to most other big container ships, these A C L vessels have stern and side doors and carry many vehicles. The ATLANTIC CAUSEWAY and ATLANTIC CONVEYOR are Cunard's contribution to the six second improved generation of ships. They are designed to carry several hundred containers together with 1,000/1,200 motor cars, roll-on roll-off traffic, heavy loads, etc.

DATA: *Owners: Cunard Line (Atlantic Container Line); Builders: Swan Hunter Shipbuilders Ltd., Walker-on-Tyne; Launched: 2 April 1969; Completed: November 1969; Tonnage (gross): 14,946; (deadweight): approx. 15,000 metric tons; Length overall: 695 ft; Breadth: 92 ft; Depth: 64 ft, Trial Speed: 24½ knots; Engines: 2 sets A.E.I. steam turbines with D.R. gearing, 38,500 s.h.p. (continuous max.); 2 boilers, 900 p.s.i., 950 deg. F; Screws: 2*

SWIFT (1969): The first international Hovercraft service was opened by Hoverlloyd in 1966. This, between Ramsgate (Pegwell Bay) and Calais is maintained by the red and white painted craft SWIFT, of the S.R.N. Mountbatten Class, and two others. Their car deck has ramps forward and aft and is flanked by two separate passenger compartments. The engines provide both hover lift and forward propulsion, the proportion of power used for each depending on weather conditions. For directional control the airscrew pylons can move 35 deg. each side of centreline.

DATA: *Owners: Hoverlloyd, London; Builders: British Hovercraft Corpn., Cowes; Entered service: 2 April, 1969; Basic weight: 110 tons; All up weight: 173 tons; Length: 130 ft. 2 ins; Breadth: 76 ft. 10 ins; Passengers: 250; Car capacity: 30; Crew: 11 (3 navigating, 4 stewardesses, 4 deck); Speed: 70 knots (max); Engines: 4 Rolls Royce Marine Proteus gas turbines, totalling 13,600 h.p. (max. continuous); Fuel load: 16 tons marine kerosene; Airscrews: 4, 19 ft. dia., variable-pitch*

SHEARWATER (1969): In addition to their passenger/car ferries, the Red Funnel Line maintains a fast hydrofoil service between Southampton and Cowes, Isle of Wight. This was opened by the H 57 type SHEARWATER, since replaced by newer craft. Hydrofoils are now employed world-wide, but prior to 1970 the SHEARWATER was the only one to maintain a regular service in the British Isles—the Channel Islands excepted.

DATA: *Owners: Southampton, Isle of Wight & S. of England R.M.S.P. Co. (Red Funnel Seaflight); Builders: Seaflight S.p.A., Messina; Entered service: 5 May, 1969; Tonnage (gross): 57; (full load displacement): 26; Length overall: 61 ft; Breadth: 15 ft. 6 ins. (26 ft. 3 ins. over foils); Draught: 8 ft. 1 in; Speed: 40 knots (32 knots service); Crew: 2; Passengers: 60; Engines: 2 x 530 h.p. Fiat diesels; Screws: 2*

QUEEN ELIZABETH 2 (1969): Commenced first transatlantic voyage from Southampton 2 May, 1969. Each passenger has on average 52% more space than on the first QUEEN ELIZABETH—over 72 sq. ft. compared with 47.75 sq. ft. At 6,000 sq. yards her open deck space is the greatest of any passenger ship. The mast serves as galley exhaust besides carrying navigational equipment. The largest liner now in commission, she combines summer North Atlantic service with off-season cruises, one of which made early 1975 took her round the world. She has 13 decks, 22 lifts, 2 bow thruster, 2 sets of stabilisers and drive-on facilities for 80 cars.

DATA: *Owners: Cunard Line Ltd; Builders: John Brown & Co; Keel laid: 4 July 1965; Launched: 20 September 1967; Tonnage (gross): 66,852; Length overall: 963 ft; Breadth: 105.3 ft; Depth: 56 ft; Draught: 32.6 ft; Service speed 28½ knots; Crew: 900; Passengers: 2,000 (less on cruises); Engines: D.R. geared turbines, 110,000 s.h.p. 3 boilers, 950 deg. F., 850 p.s.i; Screws: 2 (six bladed)*

151

ACADIA FOREST (1969): This, the world's first LASH ship (lighter aboard ship) carries her cargo in 73 lighters, each of 370 tons capacity These are loaded and discharged over the stern by a giant 510-ton travelling gantry, which straddles the 14 hatches. While at sea, other sets of lighters (one in each terminal area) are being discharged or being made ready for the next voyage. The ACADIA FOREST operates mainly from Gulf/Mississippi ports to Britain (Sheerness) and the Continent. Truly international in concept, she was ordered by Norway from Japan for long-term charter to Americans.

DATA: *Charterers: Central Gulf S.S. Corporation; Owners: T. Mosvold, Kristiansand S; Builders: Sumitomo Shipbuilding & Machinery Co., Yokosuka; Launched: 3 April, 1969; Completed: September, 1969; Tonnage (gross): 36,862; (deadweight): 43,000; Length overall: 860 ft; Breadth: 106 ft; Depth: 60 ft; Draught: 37 ft; Service speed: 19 knots (20.6 on trials); Crew: 45; Engines: One Uraga-Sulzer 9 cyl. diesel, 26,000 h.p. max. at 122 r.p.m; Screws: 1*

H.M.S. ARK ROYAL (re-commissioned 1970): The first British aircraft carrier with a steam catapult and the first with a side lift (later removed), she was re-commissioned on 24 February 1970 after a £30 million modernisation. She emerged with a bigger island and two large extensions to the flight deck; also a new waist catapult which enabled her to operate heavy all-weather Phantom strike aircraft in almost nil wind conditions. She also carries Buccaneer Mk. 2 aircraft. She is due for disposal 1978-79.

DATA: *Previous name: IRRESISTIBLE; Builders: Cammell Laird, Birkenhead; Launched: 3 May, 1950; Completed: 25 February 1955; Recommissioned: February 1970; Tonnage (full load displacement): 50,800 (43,000 standard); Length overall: 810 ft; Breadth: hull 112.8 ft. (166 ft. overall); Draught: 36 ft; Speed: 31 knots; Crew: Approx. 2,600; Engines: Parsons geared turbines, 152,000 s.h.p. 8 boilers, 400 p.s.i., 600 deg. F; Screws: 4; Armament: 4 quadruple Seacat Launchers. About 30 fixed-wing aircraft and 6 helicopters*

PACIFIC PRINCESS (1971): One of the new generation of P & O cruise liners, this handsome ship operates on the Pacific, sailing from the West coast of North America and Australia according to season. Built for Öivind Lorentzen (A/S Sea Venture) of Oslo, she was first chartered by Flagship Cruises for weekly New York—Bermuda trips. In April 1974, when so employed, she made headline news by taking off the passengers from the QE2, then immobilised by machinery trouble. Puchased by P & O late 1974, she was taken over in April 1975. The other new P & O Pacific cruise liners are the ISLAND PRINCESS and SUN PRINCESS.

154

DATA: *Owners: P & O Lines Ltd; Builders: Rheinstahl Nordseewerke, Emden; Previous name: SEA VENTURE; Launched: 9 May 1970; Completed: May 1971; Tonnage: (gross): 19,903; (deadweight): 7,200; Length overall: 553 ft. 7 ins; Breadth: 80 ft. 8 ins; Depth: 49 ft. 9 ins; Draught: 22 ft. 10 ins; Speed: 21 knots; Engines: Four 10 cyl. Fiat S.M.G. diesels, 18,000 b.h.p.; Screws: 2, plus bow thruster; Passengers: 626 open (first) class.*

DOCTOR LYKES (1972): This remarkable vessel, shown berthing at Gravesend, is one of three giant SEABEE barge carriers which operate between North European/United Kingdom ports and the U.S. Gulf. Her sisters are named ALMERIA LYKES and TILLIE LYKES. Aft, between tall side walls (open above and below), there is a 2,000-ton elevator onto which the 850-ton barges awaiting shipment are floated. Once raised, these are stowed on one of three decks which have transverse and longitudinal rails. After off-loading the barges—which can carry containers and/or break-bulk cargo—are towed to their various discharge points, sometimes far distant.

DATA: *Owners: Lykes Bros Steamship Co. Inc., New Orleans; Builders: General Dynamics Corp., Quincy, Mass.; Christened: 10 July 1971; Maiden voyage: July 1972; Tonnage (gross): 21,667; (deadweight): 38,410; Length overall: 875 ft. 11 ins; Breadth: 106 ft. 3 ins; Depth: 53 ft. 8 ins; Draught: 39 ft. 2 ins; Service Speed: 19½/20 knots; Engines: Two G.E.C. D.R. geared turbines, 36,000 s.h.p.; Screws: 1, plus bow thruster; Capacity; 38 barges, each 850 metric tons and 97 ft. 5 ins. x 35 ft; Max: 958 20 ft. containers.*

HONGKONG EXPRESS (1972): This ship is one of a 55/57,000-ton quartet employed on the North Europe—Southampton—Far East trade. For her owners they represented the third stage of their switch-over to cellular container ships. This started in 1969 with a 14,000-ton series for the U.S. trade. A year later the 27,000-ton SYDNEY EXPRESS and MELBOURNE EXPRESS were commissioned as the German contribution to the Europe—Australia container service. The others of this quartet are the BREMEN EXPRESS, HAMBURG EXPRESS and TOKIO EXPRESS. Like their British counterparts on this run they differ from previous designs in carrying some containers aft.

DATA: *Owners: Hapag-Lloyd A.G., Hamburg; Builders: Bremer Vulkan, Vegesack; Launched: 26 July 1972; Maiden voyage: November 1972; Tonnage (gross): 57,525; (deadweight): 42,222; Length overall: 941 ft. 8 ins; Breadth: 106 ft. 3 ins; Depth: 82 ft; Draught: 39 ft. 6 ins; Service Speed: 26 knots; Engines: Two Stal-Laval D.R. geared turbines, 81,000 s.h.p.; Screws: 2; Container capacity: 1,960 20 ft. units, plus 50 refrigerated.*

SHERBRO (1974): This engines-aft semi-container ship trades between the U.K. and West Africa. Variety is the keynote of her cargoes and homeward these may include aluminium, feed stuffs, cocoa, cocoa butter and shell, logs and timber. The SHERBRO has 21 derricks of 10- to 35-tons capacity and three of her four holds are served by twin hatches. The order for this ship and her two sisters, first placed by the German Schuldt Group, was later taken over by Elder Dempster Lines, the SHONGA and SHERBRO subsequently joining their fleet and the RIVER HADEJIA that of the Nigerian National Line.

DATA: *Owners: Elder Dempster Lines Ltd, Liverpool; Builders: Stocznia Szczecinska, Szczecin, Poland; Launched: 15 December 1973; Completed: March 1974; Tonnage (gross); 9,239; (deadweight) 11,900; Length overall: 477 ft. 11 ins; Breadth: 70 ft. 7 ins; Depth: 37 ft. 1 ins Draught: 27 ft. 6 ins; Service Speed: 17 knots; Engines: One Cieglski-Sulzer 6 cyl. diesel, 9,000 b.h.p.; Screws: 1, plus bow thruster; Containers: 372 20 ft. units.*

TOR BRITANNIA (1975): This magnificent blue-hulled ship was built for the Tor Line (part of the Salen Group) and is the largest and fastest yet employed on the North Sea. She operates on two routes from Gothenburg to Felixtowe and to Amsterdam, and with a sister (due 1976) she replaces the very successful TOR ANGLIA and TOR HOLLANDIA built 1966—67. She cost £13 million and in terms of design and appointments goes far beyond the conventional passenger/car ferry in being suited for possible cruising in tropical waters. On short voyages and without any alteration she can comfortably carry 700 passengers, all in two-berth cabins.

158

DATA: *Owners: A/B Tor Line, Gothenburg; Builders: Flender Werft A.G., Lubeck; Launched: 10 October 1975; Entered Service: 22 May 1975; Tonnage (gross): 15,657; (deadweight): 3,148; Length overall: 590 ft. 6 ins; Breadth: 77 ft. 7 ins; Depth: 52 ft. 8 ins; Draught: 20 ft. 4 ins; Service Speed: 24.5 knots (26 max.); Engines: Four 12 cyl. Pielstick diesels, 45,600 b.h.p.; Screws; 2, plus 2 bow thrusters; Passengers: 1,400; Vehicles: Approx. 400 cars plus 13 trailers, or 50 cars and 60 trailers.*

INDEX

The author and publishers wish to thank the following for the use of their illustrations in this book. Ministry of Defence (Crown Copyright)—113, 123, 125, 127, 140, 144, 153; The Parker Gallery—40; Science Museum, London (Crown Copyright)—11, 13, 14, 15, 16, 17, 18, 20, 21, 22, 23.